D0371369

The Dawn of the Mystical Age

The Dawn
of the
Mystical Age

by
Frank X. Tuoti

A Crossroad Book
The Crossroad Publishing Company
New York

1997
The Crossroad Publishing Company
370 Lexington Avenue, New York, NY 10017

Copyright © 1997 by Frank X. Tuoti

Grateful acknowledgment is made to the following publishers who have generously granted permission to reprint selections in this book: Shambhala Press, Boston, Mass., *Sex, Ecology, Spirituality*, by Ken Wilber ©1995; and *Living in the New Consciousness*, by Hugo Enomiya-Lassalle ©1988; Landisfarne Press, Hudson, N.Y., *The Essential Aurobindo*, ed. Robert McDermott ©1987; Ohio University Press, Athens, Oh., *The Ever-Present Origin*, by Jean Gebser © 1984; New Directions Books, New York, *New Seeds of Contemplation*, by Thomas Merton, ©1977; Quest Books, Wheaton, Ill., *Dialogues with a Modern Mystic*, by Andrew Harvey and Mark Matousek, ©1995; University of Chicago Press, Chicago, Ill., *The Future of Mankind*, by Karl Jaspers, ©1961; Paulist Press, Mahwah, N.J., *John Cassian*, The Classics of Western Spirituality, trans. Colm Luibheid, ©1985; Cistercian Publications, Spencer, Mass., offset of *The Inner Experience*, by Thomas Merton, ©1983–1984.

Printed in the United States of America

Library of Congress Cataloging-in-Publication Data

Tuoti, Frank X.
    The dawn of the mystical age / Frank X. Tuoti.
      p.   cm.
    ISBN 0-8245-1688-5 (pbk.)
    1. Mysticism. I. Title.
    BL625.T86
    291.4'22–dc21   97-15539
                                     CIP

We are standing on the border-line of the unknowable, the ineffable, and straining our eyes beyond.

–Sri Aurobindo

 # Contents

 # Acknowledgments

The author expresses his deep gratitude to Lucy Peerenboom, mother, educator, and soul-friend, who dutifully read each chapter many times as they underwent revisions, many of which were prompted by her insightful critique and suggestions.

Also to a friend of nearly a quarter-century, George A. Maloney, the Byzantine Jesuit, scholar, author, theologian, and spiritual guide, whose friendship and writings over these many years have been a continual source of inspiration. His suggestions are woven throughout this book.

Not least, to my wife, Gale, my earth, a talented artist, whose love, gentleness, and companionship constantly renew my life.

Preface: Peering into the New Consciousness

Many of the chapters of this book have their inspiration in the seminal thinking of several intellectual-spiritual giants of our century, some of whom are still living. The author acknowledges his profound indebtedness and gratitude to these "transducers of light." At the same time, I make no apology for drawing heavily on their insights for this book, while offering my own thoughts and conjectures in the bargain.

Those who are the inspiration for this book are the "see-ers" of the future, of the new mutation of consciousness that will become the revolutionary/evolutionary experience of humankind such as has not occurred in the last twenty-five hundred years. I have attempted to recast some of their writings and present them in a way that those not trained in the schools of the philosopher or the academician can readily and easily grasp. In this regard, I have carefully avoided using philosophic terminology and technical phrases found in the original works, which are, in the majority of instances, the almost exclusive domain of the specialist. A few noteworthy technical references are relegated to chapter footnotes.

At the same time, where it seemed appropriate, I offer the reader brief excerpts from the original texts, for two purposes: First, to give validity and authority to the premise of the book and to my own contributions. Second, to offer the reader a "taste" of some of the "sweet fruit" of the original writings. Ecclesiastes said there is nothing new under the sun. Pascal said that "an old idea expressed in a different way becomes a new idea." It is my hope that by recasting some of the thinking of these twentieth-century see-ers, I may have succeeded in making their thoughts "new"—and more than that, hopefully have made them accessible to a wider audience than was reached by the original publications.

The author recognizes his indebtedness to India's great modern sage Sri Aurobindo; the German Jesuit mystic and Zen master, Hugo

Enomiya-Lassalle; philosopher Karl Jaspers; mystic Andrew Harvey; once fellow Trappist Thomas Merton; quantum physicist Fritjof Captra; mystic-paleontologist Teilhard de Chardin; the "mystical doctor" Karl Rahner; philosopher Jean Gebser; Sannyasin Bede Griffiths; transpersonal psychologist Ken Wilber, Buddhists Sogyal Rinpoche and Thich Naht Hanh—and the Native American and other indigenous peoples who, unlike the West, have not sacrificed their sacred and holistic view of life on the profane altar of technological and industrial progress.

A few comments: First, whenever the word *ego* is employed, it is always used in the sense of *egocentric*, and not in the sense of ego *structure* as understood by the classic pioneers of psychology, Freud, Jung, and others. The ego is the principle that *gives unity to the mind*, without which we would be a mass of chaos incapable of even communicating with each other. Jesus and the Buddha had powerful egos but were not egocentric. Only when the ego is fully matured and integrated into the personality does egocentrism vanish—enabling the true self to emerge from the abyss of our inner depths.

Second, I have attempted to use gender-sensitive language except where to do so would appear not only awkward but possibly even absurd. There are times when use of the masculine pronoun for God is an absolute requirement, as biblical exegetes acknowledge and with which they struggle.

Third, we have called upon wisdom voices from all the great spiritual traditions, recognizing, joyfully, that no race or creed has a monopoly on truth. The arising mutation of consciousness is global and will eventually impact and advance every culture and religion.

In the final analysis—a judgment that must rest with you the reader—this book may have but one virtue to recommend it: namely, that the author has conveniently brought together between two covers the wisdom of a diverse number of sages from different cultural and spiritual traditions, and presented important aspects of their thought in an easy-to-read manner. This said, I stand with you on the shoulders of these twentieth-century Goliaths, peering excitedly with them into the future— *a future that has already arrived.*

Frank X. Tuoti
Tucson, Arizona

Part One
The Dawn of the Mystical Age

The new consciousness structure has nothing to do with might, rule or overpowering. Thus it cannot be striven for, only elicited or awakened. Anyone who strives for it, intending to attain it mentally, is condemned to failure at the outset. This is also true of those who may think that mere desire and the power of the imagination are sufficient to fully effect the new mutation.

What is needed is care, a great deal of patience, and the laying aside of many preconceived notions, wishful dreams, and the blind sway of demands. There is a need for a certain detachment towards oneself and the world.

—Jean Gebser[1]

1 🌿 Home, Home to Eden

That is what I am made for; I am made for Eden.

—Thomas Merton

Humankind is on the path to enlightenment. We are the people of the Quantum Leap! In spite of the enormous evil, appalling suffering and the dark forces that today hold much of humanity in their grip, this is a book about hope and radiant expectations for the future. It alludes to the real prospect of a world that will be spiritually endowed and spiritually charged and ordered. Looking back over past ages, light has always emerged out of darkness.

This book is about the *transcendence* of the human race and the *now-developing mutation of higher consciousness* which, when more fully realized by humankind, will necessarily bring about equality, justice, and peace. Justice in all its manifestations will be one of the marks of the emerging epoch. This book is about the passing of what is called The Mental Age and the onset of The Mystical Age, an age during which man and woman will become mystics.

It is about our embarkation into the Fourth (Spiritual) Dimension (Einstein's term), wherein the noteworthy achievements and accomplishments of the Mental Age will be not discarded but, rather, integrated into the new consciousness, thus raising the existing consciousness structure to a new and higher level.

It is about the rediscovery of the Sacred Feminine, whose powers are the subject of much of this book. It is about our Motherly God's abundant compassion and exceeding great mercy, and about the coming "sacred marriage" between patriarchy and matriarchy and its progeny.

Who shall bring His message?
I am waiting for the moment
When the touchstone of the new dawn
Shall turn this earth to gold.

3

The New Age is heralded with the call:
"Open, open the door! Let darkness perish,
And lustre, born of sorrow and pain,
Shine forth in you."
                                            —Rabindranath Tagore[1]

Over recent decades a foreboding darkness has descended upon
earth, different perhaps from that of primordial creation when "there
was darkness over the deep" (Gen. 1:1), but a darkness nonetheless
that is its modern-day equivalent. Our great and only hope is the reality that God's Spirit still hovers over us. The Divine Mercy still broods
over the chaotic waters of our inner depths, and our planet itself
remains the garden of the divine delight—now writhing, stupefied and
clueless, in a self-inflicted agony.

The greatest darkness is not the blatant evil clearly to be observed
but the corruption and debasement of the human spirit by which
modern humanity has deliberately chosen shallowness and superficiality to be its dominant characteristics. Reduced to a word, we
have chosen suicide. "The greatest of all vices," wrote Oscar Wilde,
"is superficiality."

> Sometimes I think that the greatest achievement of modern culture is
> its brilliant selling of samsara (ignorance and illusion), and its barren
> distractions. Modern society seems to me a celebration of all the things
> that lead away from the truth, make truth hard to live for, and dis-
> courage people from even believing that it exists.
>   —Tibetan Master Sogyal Rinpoche[2]

We have raged against wisdom; we have converged the Light with
a bushel basket. The words of the Nazarene ring true—we prefer the
darkness, which we have made our cozy cocoon, out of which we
refuse to emerge. Modern men and women not only have little experience of the unconscious but live unconsciouslessly. We have blotted
out every trace of the sacred, the numinous; we have drained both
humanity and nature from any ultimate meaning.

The shallow pools where twentieth-century *homo erectus* presently
congregates en masse—like schools of aimless, darting minnows—have
become the spawning ground of our present moral and environmen-
tal catastrophe. These festering shoals, fed not by the clean springs

of life but by diseased rivulets carrying our obituary notices, have become the poisoned habitat of every kind of evil, the polluted birthing pools of our infirm and fractured world. We have made ourselves homeless wanderers in the desert of our despair.

> O homeless wanderer,
> The soundless melody resounds in your march.
> Do you hear the Infinite Beyond incessantly?
> Her love is terrible,
> Therefore you are homeless.
>
> —Tagore

These pages attempt to survey the reality, promises, and characteristics of the developing Mystical Age. *Our return to Eden is the evolving event of the Mystical Age,* an age that has already dawned upon us, issuing out of a new breakthrough in the relentless march of human evolution. However presently embryonic, it brings with it an ascending transformation of consciousness such as the human race has not hitherto undergone.

Though presently realized by a relative few, this higher consciousness has already "descended" upon a diverse number of spiritually gifted people, transcending religious, ethnic and geographical boundaries. They are the heralds of this new grace-charged epoch, the forerunners of an age being invited to return to a primordial state of wisdom, unitive consciousness, and the recovery of the sacred. At this stage of the evolutionary turn of the wheel, many, if not most, people will not be able to accept such an "unreasonable" message. There are those not ready to embrace or comprehend things proposed in this book:

> Explain (the new consciousness) to someone on the rational level and all you get, at best, is that deer "caught-in-the-headlights" blank stare or, at worst, you get something like "and did we forget to take our Prozac today?"
>
> —Ken Wilber[3]

No new structure of consciousness can ever be realized immediately. It will take indefinite spans of time before the new mutation of consciousness and its integration make their way into the mainstream of humanity. But let us know with certainty that, whether or not you and I enter into it, the "dance of evolution" will go on with or without us. It is our choice.

If you are convinced that the foregoing is something of a pipe dream, it might be best to put this book back on the shelf. If you are at least intrigued, please read on with an open mind. If you are already convinced of this book's message, I invite you to spread the "good news" of the unfolding Mystical Age and the consequential rediscovery of the Sacred Feminine, the womb of our rebirth.

As proposed by the title of my former book, *Why Not Be a Mystic?*, we are all called to become mystics (people of the fourth spiritual dimension), or remain imprisoned in what Sri Aurobindo calls the "commonplace experience of man," or in Karl Rahner's words, "to be nothing at all."

Enlightened gurus, Christian and non-Christian, must lead us out of our present chaos and disorientation and point the way back to Eden. Such "agents of transformation" are "sprouting" all around us. Shall we seriously listen to them—or, like the Israelites of old, will we stone our prophets? This book is an effort to realize the hope and vision of Sri Aurobindo:

> The coming of the spiritual age must be preceded by the appearance of an increasing number of individuals who are no longer satisfied with the normal intellectual, vital and physical existence of man, but perceive that a greater evolution is the real goal of humanity and attempt to effect it in themselves, lead others to it, and make it the recognized goal of the race.
>
> In proportion as they succeed, and to the degree they carry this evolution, the yet unrealized potentiality which they represent will become an actual possibility of the future.
>
> —Sri Aurobindo[4]

2   Humanity on the Precipice

Either mankind will physically perish, or there will be a change in the moral-political condition of man. If we grow sure of our freedom, and thus of our responsibility, there is a chance for a change, and thus salvation. The change itself involves a new way of thinking.

—Karl Jaspers[1]

Although flares of light have begun to appear on the horizon, we must, at the same time, prepare for the real possibility of still greater darkness, more intense and widespread suffering and greater desolation and destruction visiting our planet. The Mystical Age is offered us with no absolute guarantee that "all will be well" in time to forestall and reverse the course of our psychotic self-destruction. At this point in the evolutionary sweep, humankind hangs tenuously on the precipice, the most precarious balancing act yet to confront the human race. "Mankind," wrote Teilhard de Chardin, "is being taken to the point where it will have to choose between suicide or adoration."

As we peer into the future—the very *immediate* future—we must anticipate worldwide convulsive earth changes—huge volcanic eruptions, earthquakes, and floods that decimate large land areas, and deadly new microbes that mutate out of reach of known vaccines and antidotes. We have just about run out of antidotes. The one antidote that remains to us, a perennial one, is a spiritual revolution induced by a rising transformation of consciousness.

It is certainly valid to believe that Mother Earth, in some mysterious way, is purifying herself and making ready for a new beginning. But more than this, she is giving us stern warnings in an attempt to bring us to our senses. Her "anger" is not a form of punishment and retribution, but mercy calling us to repent of our destructive, hedonistic, suicidal ways.

If man and the earth are unable to endure the tensions, they will be torn apart by them. Both will perish in their present form and, after the intervening breathing spell, a new earth and a new era will arise.

—Jean Gebser[2]

We can reasonably entertain the hope that humanity will not again be caught up in the convulsive destructiveness of another global war. Then again, our hope may disappoint. If the latter is to be our fate, it will be self-induced. The "gods" will not have failed us; rather, we shall have failed the gods. Einstein's words should give us pause for somber reflection: "I do not know what weapons will be used in a forthcoming war; but the one waged after that will be fought by bows and arrows."

Everything depends on us, on you and on me, on our decision to participate—or not—in what is being offered us. We must not surrender to the fatalistic idea that because we are "just one individual" we can do nothing to influence a future that is teeter-tottering on the precipice. Each one of us is a free individual, with the power to influence larger spheres and activities of the human family. Each one of us has the power to effect change, by becoming more truly human. *Being blooms! Being radiates! Being is contagious!* Unnoticed, *being* penetrates and mysteriously touches hearts. Unobserved, the manifested truth of our inner being, joined with others, can transform our world.

> However powerless we feel, no one is wholly powerless. However a minute quantity, the individual may be among the factors that make history, for each is a factor. The individual cannot attribute it all to a tide of events of which none of it is his doing.
>
> —Karl Jaspers[3]

A continent away, the words of Karl Jaspers are echoed by India's great twentieth century sage:

> The change from the mental ... to the spiritual order of life must necessarily be accomplished in the individual, and in a great number of individuals before it can lay effective hold upon the community. All great changes find their clear and effective power and their direct shaping force in the mind and spirit of an individual, or a limited number of individuals.
>
> —Sri Aurobindo[4]

Nevertheless, we run the risk that, as we look out upon the widespread suffering and desolation all around us, we may fall into apathy and even terminal despair, which will only accelerate our hell-bent rush to global suicide. We must work diligently while we hope confidently; we must grasp the hand of mercy which is always extended toward us as we pray: "Thy will be done."

Though the evolutionary upward spiral is relentless and "undefeatable," we must not think of it in mechanistic, deterministic terms —as sprinting ahead at a fixed predetermined velocity. Rather, the velocity by which evolution will attain its ultimate ordained goal will be determined by the choices we humans make, one by one and collectively. How well and how faithfully we interact with the galaxy of graces being showered upon us, now and over the oncoming decades, will determine whether our inheritance will be effulgent light or damning darkness.

> There must be individuals who are able to see, to develop, to re-create themselves in the image of the Spirit and to communicate both their idea and its power to the mass. There must be...a society, a communal mind...ready to follow.
>
> —Sri Aurobindo[5]

At the same time, India's great sage gives us a warning:

> There are moments when the Spirit moves among men and the breath of the Lord is abroad upon the waters of our being. Unhappy is the man or nation which, when the divine moment arrives, is found sleeping or unprepared to use it, because the lamp has not been kept trimmed for the welcome. But thrice woe to them who strong and ready, yet waste the force or misuse the moment. Let not worldly prudence whisper too closely in thy ear, for it is the hour of the unexpected.
>
> —Sri Aurobindo[6]

We are co-creators of our own destiny. This power to co-create our future is accompanied by the benevolence of endless choices and opportunities offered us to return to our Eden home. What deeply yearns to burst free in us is *itself* the Eden we seek. The journey we must take is an interior one, one we take "standing still."

As Thomas Merton remarked at the closing of a prayer conference in Calcutta, "We must become what we already are." The divine spark

burning within the deepest core of us all is close to becoming asphyx-
iated. The voice crying out in the wilderness of our desolated depths
grows ever weaker, ever fainter. What will happen if enough of us do
not hear the Voice pleading to be heard, pleading to save us?

Jesus told his disciples: "Behold, the kingdom of God is within you—it
is here." What counts is the reality of the eternal, the way of life and
action, as encompassing immortality. This presence of eternity may
result in mankind's rescue from suicide. And in this presence, even if
reason and existence fail, hope will remain.

—Karl Jaspers[7]

3 ❧ Out of the Darkness

In the present crisis we should not forget that, in the past, the downfall of a consciousness structure was always, at the same time, a sign and even a hidden guarantee of an upcoming (new) structure. When modern man is able to gain some inkling of what is meant by this new dimension, he will be able to breathe easier.

—Hugo Enomiya-Lassalle[1]

If we properly understand Eden to be not a physical, historic place of human habitation, but a dwelling place of God's special presence, we can then accept and understand that a return to Eden is indeed possible. Out of the darkness and desolation of humanity's own heart, a light is clearly beginning to shine. The present gradual uplifting of humankind into the spiritual Fourth Dimension is, in a real and vital sense, a return to Eden.

Eden is sometimes equated in the Bible with the "Garden of God," where the perfection of humankind is found:

> You, Zion, were an exemplar of perfection, full of wisdom, perfect in beauty. You were in Eden, in the Garden of God.
>
> —Ezek. 28:31

> Yea, Yahweh has pity on Zion and turns her desolation into Eden, her wasteland into the Garden of Yahweh. Joy and gladness shall be found in her, thanksgiving, and the sound of music.
>
> —Isa. 51:3

In its spiritual estrangement from God, humanity is being called anew to live in the "Garden of Yahweh" and to know "joy and gladness." This special state of consciousness is situated in the human heart, in the hidden ground of love. Hearts are being touched by a merciful, loving God who broods over us to recreate us—just as God's *ruah* once brooded over the chaotic waters at the dawn of creation. The divine *ruah*, the sacred breath and spirit, is even now breathing

11

the light of higher consciousness into diverse human hearts, without respect for race, creed, geography, or ethnic origins. No new technologies, no Internet or Cyberspace manipulations, no marvelous drug can rescue us from the grip of our crisis—only a return to Eden.

> The dilemma of earth and mankind today will not be resolved by some sort of human machination. The dilemma will be resolved only by the full realization of the present consciousness mutation.
>
> —Jean Gebser[2]

In the past, going as far back as can be accurately accessed, humankind has always been rescued from its dilemma just as it was about to crash:

> Mutations (of consciousness) have always appeared when the prevailing consciousness structures proved no longer adequate for mastering the world. In our day, the rationalistic, deficient mental structure presents an equal threat, and the breakthrough into the integral will also bring about a new and decisive mutation.
>
> —Hugo Enomiya-Lassalle[3]

A fallacy exists which insists that our predicament is caused by loss of religion, by greed and materialism, adoration of technology, and the like. This is not so. These are only symptoms of the transitional distress of our times, not the root causes. The demon beneath all this is the deterioration of our present mental consciousness structure, which for several centuries has been continually decaying. Only the emergence and integration of the new consciousness will dispel the darkness of our present obsolete mental-rational consciousness and rescue us from our shallowness and fascination with the trivial and superficial.

The time has long since passed when any one spiritual tradition can boast that it possesses a monopoly on truth. As St. Anselm once commented: "Do not be concerned where you find truth, for it all comes from the same source." There is an anonymous saying that hangs by a piece of tape on the wall of my den and reads:

> Our first task in approaching another people, another culture, another religion is to take off our shoes, for the place we are approaching is holy. Else we may find ourselves treading on another's dream. More serious still, we may forget that God was there before our arrival.

To which we can add the words of Hugo Enomiya-Lassalle:

> The new consciousness is a remedy against the erroneous claim to the exclusive possession of the truth by any one creed, which has been the source of so much harm.[4]

Dr. Jonas Salk, who discerned the dawning of a new evolutionary epoch, said that when "critical mass" is reached, when a sufficient number of people have been gifted with higher consciousness, the Mystical Age will have profound and wide-ranging consequences that will transform and spiritualize our planet. To the extent that we enter into the Fourth Dimension, and to the degree that we open ourselves to the Spirit being poured out anew upon us, will the Mystical Age unfold into fullness.

The structure of three-dimensional mental consciousness, which still dominates our time, even as the mystical-intuitive new consciousness is simultaneously arising, is obsolete and no longer valid. Its obsolescence is verified in the material world by the scientific discoveries of quantum physics and quantum mechanics, while the writings of great mystics of our time assure us—with a certitude at least as valid as the scientific model—that we have indeed entered upon a new consciousness structure, the Mystical Age.

While it is not possible to precisely predict the exact nature of events this new epoch will bring as it unfolds, the attributes and characteristics of this new stage in humanity's development can be generally anticipated and broadly sketched out. The second part of this book represents the author's attempt to depict, however incompletely, some of the salient marks and characteristics of the unfolding Mystical Age. Some of these pages endeavor to point to the path we must take and the choices we must courageously make if we are to enter the Fourth Dimension and become shareholders of its legacy.

> Everyone of us, in his or her own way, wherever we may be, is not only a witness but an instrument of what is to be reality—hence the necessity for us to create the means with which we ourselves can jointly shape this new reality.
>
> —Jean Gebser[5]

These pages point to a spiritual journey "into our Deep," into the mystery of our inner self, which we must undertake if survival and not suicide is to be our fate.

In the Dark and the Deep there are truths which can always heal. We might have lost the Light . . . but what is even more frightening, we have lost the Mystery and the Deep . . . and lost it in a world dedicated to surface and shadows, to exteriors and shells, whose prophets lovingly exhort us to dive into the shallow end of the pool head first.

—Ken Wilber[6]

4 ✿ Image and Likeness

God said: "Let us make humankind in our image, according to our likeness. . . ." So God created humankind in his image, in the image of God he created them, male and female he created them.

—Gen. 1:26-27

Against the false doomsday prophets of the Christian fundamentalists who prophesy the imminent end and consummation of the world, the great wisdom teachers of Christianity and other traditions herald the emergence of humankind into a new and exciting epoch: the Mystical Age.

Typical of the present situation is the widespread discussion about a final cataclysm spelling world destruction. Many comfort themselves in the hope that we shall be able somehow to carry on after emigrating to some far-flung star, when this time we shall not make the same mistakes. This accounts for the interest in various religious (fundamentalist) prophecies about the end of the world.

—Enomiya-Lassalle[1]

In his masterpiece *The Ever-Present Origin,* philosopher Jean Gebser makes the observation that pessimism and defeatism are almost always the prevailing view of humankind in transition:

Anyone today who considers the emergence of a new era of mankind as a certainty . . . seems unlikely to realize the possibility of a transition . . . or evince any readiness to take a leap into tomorrow. Such a reaction, the reaction of a mentality headed for a fall, is only too typical of man in transition.[2]

Such a vision for humankind is met by a cynical and even morbid attitude that sees humankind spiraling not upward but downward. This is not the view held by the great sages and cutting-edge thinkers of our "age in transition." Rather, in this new evolutionary epoch, *already begun,* the mystical life, with its many attendant gifts will eventfully become the new milieu and the new paradigm. Authentic, God-imbued mysticism is a reality already blossoming about us:

> Mysticism is a phenomenon that has rapidly swept through the world during the latter part of the twentieth century, and will surely continue to increase as we enter the third millennium.
>
> —George A. Maloney[3]

We are witnesses to the ultimate task of consciousness, to be the vehicle for God's becoming fully conscious in creation—what may be called the "concretion of spirituality."

It is to the Greek church fathers, particularly St. Basil the Great, that we owe the theological distinction between "image" and "likeness." The image of God remains whole and intact within us. Our likeness to God, however, has become warped and distorted, the cause of all our dysfunctions. The "divine spark" (Meister Eckhart) still burns ceaselessly within us. Like a gas stove's glowing pilot light, it awaits the moment when it is *invited* and *permitted* to burst into a transforming flame. The recovery of our likeness to the Divine, our divinization, is what is called "the spiritual journey." We must go back from whence we came—back to Eden.

In this new era, an ever-increasing number will become masters of their passions and emotions, approaching the state of *apatheia*, or "passionlessness," of which the Greek church fathers wrote.[5] Our passions, good in themselves, will remain, but they will no longer hold such destructive sway over us. Humankind will become less unstable and violent, therefore more peaceful and more inwardly free. Humankind is on the path of recovering, through gifted grace, through wisdom, its pristine state of being—the restoration of its likeness of God.

Extraordinary as it may sound, I believe, with others, that the mercy and grace of God, boundless in their richness, will lead us through the horrendous evil and human desolation so evident all around us. Other times and other ages have experienced evil and horror comparable to our own, but lacking our modern network of instantaneous global communications, were not aware of their full extent. Each such age, like the phoenix, rose up out of the ashes, and humankind continued on the road to its ordained destiny, the next evolutionary advance towards the Omega point.

In our present crisis we should not forget that, in the past, the downfall of a consciousness structure was always, at the same time, a sign and even a hidden guarantee of an upcoming (new) structure.

—Enomiya Lassalle[4]

Humanity, as Merton observed, is on a new river, a new collective journey carrying us ever closer to fulfilling our innate potential as spirit-impregnated, God-endowed human beings. We have entered the Fourth Dimension, a new mutation of consciousness—*already present within us*—awaiting the time of its fruition. Shortly before his death, the German Jesuit mystic and Zen Master Hugo Enomiya-Lassalle wrote: "When humankind has integrated the fourth dimension, humanity will have achieved enlightenment."[5] If we respond and contribute our cooperative part, the Mystical Age will carry us over the final confining boundary of our present Mental Age—which Andrew Harvey has called "the concentration camp of reason" (but still the present dominant paradigm)—and transport us over the barbed-wire fences of purely rational, analytical thinking to mystical-intuitive thinking. In this new era we will begin to live *time-free*, freed from the anarchy and chains of "clock time" by learning to live in the present moment.

We must be clear about several aspects of this new eon: First, it will not happen "Pentecost-like," of a sudden, but will gradually unfold and become integrated over many decades, perhaps centuries, as did the Axial Age of some 2,500 years ago. Second, the rational mind will not be simply rejected as we evolve from the Mental to the Mystical Age, but will be integrated into it and will serve the new consciousness. Third, not all will become enlightened, but only those who respond to the Divine Mother's gift and call, who courageously strive to lead authentic, mindful, compassionate, centered lives.

The great contributions and accomplishments of past ages will not be discarded and thrown upon the scrap heap of history, but will be integrated into a new wholeness and completeness. On the purifying waves of an emerging enlightened consciousness, humankind will once again, as in times that marked the first appearance of humanity upon earth, rise to honor the sacred, and offer thanksgiving and praise to the Divine Mother. Humankind, once again, will be imbued with a sacred view of life and the cosmos. *A return to the Sacred Feminine will be the womb of our new birth.*

The streams of Heaven shall murmur in her laugh,
Her lips shall be the honeycombs of God,
Her limbs his golden jars of ecstasy,
Her breasts the rapture-flowers of Paradise.
She shall bear Wisdom in her voiceless bosom,
Strength shall be with her like a conqueror's sword
And from her eyes the Eternal bliss shall gaze.

—Sri Aurobindo[6]

5 ❦ A New River

We are on a new river, but we don't know it.

—Thomas Merton

Every great religious tradition of East and West will be impacted and changed as the ascending dawn of the Mystical Age bathes the world in new light. Most affected will be those traditions most rigidly structured and systematized, for such confining structures will not be able to withstand the relentless force of the new intuitive-mystical fourth-dimensional thinking. Humanity, in the words of Enomiya-Lassalle, will experience the transparency of life, "a transparency which penetrates words and concepts to the very essence of things and which is not the result of rational deduction."[1] The whole world is open and transparent; only *we* are closed.

> The magic spring
> where Khezr once drank the water of life
> is in your own home—
> but you have blocked its flow.

—Fahkruddin ʿIraqi[2]

More than other, less-systematized religions, Christianity will be greatly impacted and changed. It will undergo a structural mutation that will greatly liberate its adherents, allowing the Spirit, which heretofore has been severely constrained by conventional ways of thinking and excessive authoritarian control, to "blow where it will." (See chapter "A New Church.")

> Christianity will probably be more seriously affected by the integration of the new consciousness than most other religions. What Christianity will look like after the total integration of the new consciousness among humanity is something no one can foretell at present.

—Enomiya-Lassalle[3]

From this perspective, Christianity has the most to gain as the future unfolds. The seeds of change were quietly planted over a quarter-century ago by visionary and sage Pope John XXIII. Try as some might, these seeds cannot be dug up and stamped out. Their destiny is to bloom fully in the Mystical Age.

Of necessity, the old wineskin must be discarded; only a new wineskin will be able to contain the new wine of fourth-dimensional consciousness now being poured out—this "best wine" being saved for last. A new vintage, which is actually the pristine *original* vintage, will replace the *vin du jour*, the wine of the day.

> The conceptual representation of religious truths is no longer sufficient even for upright Christians. Many of these people no longer look to theology for healing; they turn rather to different ways of experiencing God for themselves.
>
> —Enomiya-Lassalle[4]

The Church will undergo considerable pain and anguish as it moves into the new age, as is already occurring. As the new mutation evolves and as staid, centuries-old structures disintegrate, column by column, the Church will experience dislocation and distress, including the defection of multitudes of the so-called faithful, a decline already well in process.

The slow, ongoing crucifixion of existing rationalistic and categorical thinking will pierce all the ligaments of the Church, which, as Karl Rahner foresaw, will become declericalized to a great extent. This "declericalization" of the Church must not be misinterpreted. Some offices must remain in the Church with certain functions and powers if the Church is to escape chaos. The declericalization of the Church will demand more of a shift in consciousness than changes in the organizational structure, although that too must also come to pass:

> As soon as these obvious dogmatic truths [of the Church] are lived and practised impartially and taken for granted by office-holders and other Christians, then we [will] have what we call a declericalized Church: that is a Church in which the office-holders too in joyous humility allow for the fact that the Spirit breathes where it will and that he has not arranged an exclusive and permanent tenancy with them. They [must] recognize that the charismatic element, which can never be completely

regulated, is just as necessary as office in the church. That office is never identical with the Spirit, which can never be replaced.

—Karl Rahner[5]

Without this shift in consciousness, the old structures will remain substantially intact. The ponderous, multilayered central bureaucracy of the Catholic Church—unparalleled in any of the other world religions—is destined to gradually mutate. Although the "power-possessed" will fight tooth and nail to retain the status quo, they cannot succeed. No new Pentecost can dawn on the countryside of medieval thinking. What is authentic and real will be preserved, carried forward, and integrated. What is obsolete and the spiritless carrion of another age will be left to be picked apart by scavengers, feasting hopelessly on dry bones.

It is always the Church's task to carry over that which remains forever ... into a new form more appropriate to the present and future than the form now slowly but inevitably crumbling, and thus to hand on this permanent reality authentically and effectively to the coming age.

—Karl Rahner[6]

Just as many Christians denied their faith in the early centuries of persecution (more than we would like to believe), so will many leave "the faith" over coming decades—those who cannot see past the apparent unraveling of the present church to the ensuing new Pentecost. Those who remain will be people of deep faith and prayer; many will be mystics. In the vision of Karl Rahner, these remnants of "experiential believers" (Rahner's "Church of the Little Flock") will one day reignite the church, and re-create a truly spiritual church.

For the new Pentecost to occur, Christianity must return to its roots, to the life and teachings of Jesus and those who walked with him on this earth. The scriptures must be approached in a "spiritual" way. There must be more meditative *listening* than intellectual reading, more prayerful *silence* than exegetical analyzing, more *openness of heart* than closed rational thinking. The hidden, mystical meaning of scripture must be recovered, as in days gone by:

While attending to the divine reading, seek the hidden sense which is present in most passages of the divine Scriptures. For these words which are written are the forms of certain mysteries, the image of divine things.

—Origen[7]

The Christian must come profoundly and intimately close to Christ; come to know him in our silence and, in some way, enter into *his* silence, into the silence that is both the womb and ground of his words and teachings. Then will scripture become "spirit and life" (John 6:63) and become integrated into the new consciousness, birthing a more illumined truth that will truly set us free.

As we search for our Christian roots and the teachings of Christ, Enomiya-Lassalle asks, "How can we be assured that our search will reveal the authentic teaching and experience of Christ?" He answers: "If there is any assurance, it can only lie in the individual religious experience encountered in deep prayer and contemplation."[8] As the new consciousness takes root, the great religions of the world will come together in a new harmony of reconciliation, understanding, and cooperation. We will share the riches of our traditions with one another and learn from one another, understanding that which manifests itself in different ways, in different historical-cultural settings. There will arise a new unity of humankind, based not on economics or "self defense" but on a new spirit of cooperation, understanding, respect, and mutual admiration arising out of humanity's search for truth.

This we see happening already, as those who are conversant with present interreligious dialogue can attest. Because of this, those rooted in their particular traditions will become better disciples of their chosen spiritual paths. The Native American, the Aborigine, and other marginalized peoples will be recognized for their perennial wisdom and will be listened to by "civilization" perhaps for the first time. All will share in the uplifting of humankind's spirit and aspirations.

The genuine irruption of the other side into this side, the presence of the beyond in the here and now, of the transcendent in the immanent, of the divine in the human (will) become transparent.

—Jean Gebser[9]

6   Signs of the Now-Present Future

In this second (patriarchal) stage, humankind left the womb of the Mother, and developed extraordinary powers of manipulation and domination. It depended for much of its energy on a denial of our fundamental connectedness to each other.

—Andrew Harvey[1]

We have said that it is not possible to predict specific events or to assign even general dates to the unfolding tableau of the Mystical Age. It will be possible to pinpoint such signs (and wonders) only in retrospect, after they have emerged from the mist of what can now be only a blurred future. Nonetheless, we are witness to a number of signs that have already appeared, giving evidence that we are indeed destined to be "the people of the quantum leap."

The discovery of quantum physics/mechanics, which has revolutionized our concept of the cosmos and the workings of the material order, is one such manifestation that a new epoch has dawned. The static laws of Newtonian physics, which viewed all elements of the universe as disconnected, independent entities, has given way to the insight that all creation is a vast, single web of interconnectedness and interdependence. The cosmos is one, and we are one with it. One for all and all *in* one.

The "invention" of cyberspace is a development unparalleled in human history, a planetary "unifying field" of yet-to-be-realized power and potential. Cyberspace is transforming worldwide communication and accelerating the transmission of knowledge of every kind at "warp speed." It may be the most important advance in human evolution since the invention of writing. It will make great contributions to evolutionary advancement.

As the world merges closer and closer together, truly a global village, so the great religions of the world are coming together in fruitful dialogue, in the serious pursuit of mutual understanding, respect, even admiration. Dramatic evidence of this was the historic Christian–Buddhist encounter held in July 1996 at "my old Kentucky home," the Abbey of Gethsemani. For almost a full week, the Dalai Lama and several Tibetan monks met with Catholic monks and religious, sharing their teachings, traditions, and insights; meditating together; and reaching out to each other in friendship. Such an event would not have been possible twenty-five or thirty years ago. A light is shining in the darkness.

During the 1960s, an event called Vatican II shook the Catholic world, an earthquake of sorts, whose tremors would be felt not only in Catholicism but in latitudes and longitudes well removed from the Church. The vision of the Second Vatican Council has yet to be fully realized (mutations of higher consciousness take time!), but will be fully validated and integrated as the Church moves into the now-present future.

In the chapter "The Emergence of Women," we investigate the history and status of women. The yoke of patriarchy and male domination has begun to be lifted, and women are being released from the heavy burden imposed by male "testosterone-itis." The backs of women, bent over under the weight of male-imposed oppression, are straightening; women are beginning to stand tall. The struggle, which is global—and therefore a mark of a new epoch—is far from over, but it too will taste final victory in the developing now-present future.

The foregoing are but some of the signs that a new evolutionary epoch has surely dawned. Like Sri Aurobindo, we too sense that humanity is on the "borderline of the unknowable, the ineffable." We too "strain our eyes beyond."

> I know that Thy creation cannot fail,
>   even through the mists of mortal thought.
> Infallable are Thy mysterious steps,
>   and though Necessity dons the garb of Chance
> hidden in the blind shifts of Fate, she keeps
> the slow calm logic of Infinity's pace,
> and the inviolate sequence of its will.
>
> —Sri Aurobindo[2]

7 &. The Present Great Planet Earth

> We face a danger, due to cumulative effects, that may extend to lethal contamination of the whole atmosphere, of the destruction of mankind, of life itself.
>
> —Karl Jaspers[1]

Some forty years have passed since Rachel Carson's *Silent Spring* sounded the alarm that the world was rushing headlong to its ruination—not by the detonation of some super hydrogen bomb, nor by the collision with earth of a giant asteroid such as that supposed to have killed off the dinosaurs—but by "we the people," who, in our blind, arrogant pride, have poisoned the very Mother Earth which now agonizingly strains to sustain us.

> The thin layer of soil that forms a patchy covering over the continents controls our own existence and that of every animal of the land. Life not only formed the soil, but other living things of incredible abundance and diversity. By their presence and by their activities the myriad organisms of the soil make it capable of supporting the earth's green mantle.
>
> —Rachel Carson[2]

Earth's green mantle has turned a dingy gray since Rachel Carson first penned those words. Many highly respected scientific voices say that we have perhaps twenty-five years, fifty at the outside, in which to reverse the tide of destruction that grips our world. To use a popular idiom, the "window of opportunity" is narrow and closing fast. Unless we act now, with enlightened vigor, it will slam shut before our bewildered, disbelieving eyes.

> The earth does not belong to man; man belongs to the earth. This we know. All things are connected like blood which unites one family. Whatever befalls the earth befalls the sons of the earth. Man did not

25

weave the web of life; he is merely a strand in it. Whatever he does to
the web, he does to himself.

–Chief Seattle[3]

Is Mother Earth rising up to purify herself, preparing to cleanse
herself in preparation for a new beginning? Many think so. Earthquakes and massive floods have become more numerous and destructive over recent years. What is called the Pacific Ring of Fire is now
much more violently active as the Pacific plate continues to shift con-
vulsively, as if writhing in agony. Volcanic eruptions of enormous pro-
portions may darken the sky with their ashen discharge. Our rain
forests are being destroyed at the rate of one football-sized area every
hour; new and deadly microbes are surfacing and threatening to
migrate. The hole in the ozone layer is now almost twice the size of
Europe and getting larger. Meanwhile, the military is experimenting
with powerful contrivances deliberately blowing holes in the ozone
layer. Humanity, indeed, is its own most lethal enemy.

> The process of disintegration of which we are contemporary witness
> will take on various forms, deformities which will engulf the entire
> earth and mankind with unprecedented degrees of terror. If the spiri-
> tual strength that is new to us (present mutation) has not been per-
> ceived until then, the suffering and anxieties of our day will have been
> in vain.
>
> –Jean Gebser[4]

Respected seismologists concur that such a scenario is probable.
There are those who see a period of darkness covering the earth,
such as the Bible foretells. Spiritual leaders of many Native American
peoples have independently had visions of the near future, revealing
a period of global purification. Mother Earth, they predict, will rebel
and begin to cleanse herself by means of catastrophic upheavals.

As we look back to ancient times, we are tempted to think nostal-
gically that our ancestors possessed an "ecological wisdom" not
shared by us. This simply is not so. Ancient peoples would deplete the
soil used for farming and then move on to another area where deple-
tion would begin all over again. Then on to the next area, until the
land was used up. However, they lacked the "efficient" means we have
today with which to inflict their "innocent ignorance" on vast areas

of the planet. The main difference between tribal times and our own is that today we have at our disposal monstrous earth-devouring machines and killing chemicals that can quickly wipe out huge areas of forest, plant, and animal life. Our rivers, streams, and oceans are being defiled with our toxins. Entire animal species are disappearing week by week.

> To destroy a living species is to silence a part of God's voice in our universe. God's logos, in whom all things are created, will no longer speak to us about God's beauty and loving presence in such creatures.
>
> —George A. Maloney[5]

The deterioration of our planet is directly rooted in the pollution of humanity's spirit, poisoned by greed, lust for power, and the voracious appetite of the West for luxury and comfort, regardless of what it has cost Mother Earth or others. The "culture of death" proclaimed by Pope John Paul II is at the root of the world's diseased state. The Dalai Lama and sages of other great spiritual traditions say likewise. The Native American has said it for almost a century.

The great religions of the world have largely failed us and, in many ways, have contributed to our plight. Christianity has long distorted the words of Genesis whereby God endowed humankind with the responsibility to be stewards, not capacious masters, of the earth. Christianity, the dominant religion of the West, has done little over recent decades to sound the alarm and work to effect change. It has sometimes sided with the purveyors of destruction in the interest of "progress."

Like Christianity, the great traditions of the East too are the offspring of the patriarchal age:

> A long tragic imbalance of the masculine has brought humankind to the moment when, unless it recovers the feminine powers of the psyche—of intuition, patience, reverence for nature, knowledge of the holy unity of things—and marries these powers to the masculine energies of will, reason, passion for order and control, life will end on the planet.
>
> —Andrew Harvey[6]

The Christianity of Christ, the Buddhism of the Buddha, and the spirituality of the Hindu Vedas have become diluted with the shuffle of the centuries, the farther away we get from their founders. (Before he died, Francis of Assisi saw his vision for the Franciscan Friars largely disintegrate, reduced to a "more practical vision" by the rationalists and pragmatists.) Over the decades, greed and short-sighted opportunism have overtaken mystical wisdom and enlightened vision, stampeded under foot by our compulsion to dominate, consume, and accumulate. Yet, in spite of everything, in the face of an apparent on-rushing apocalyptic future, we must not weakly yield to pessimism. There is reason for us to be prophets of hope and optimism and not ominous oracles of despair. Despair and fatalistic resignation are the easy paths of reacting to crises, the marks of defeatists. Courage, hope, and determination to overcome are the marks of the human person at his and her best.

The mercy of the Divine Mother is without limit and infinitely beyond our capacity to even remotely comprehend. She broods over us with tender concern, as a mother gazes anxiously upon a deathly ill child. She longs to come to our aid with the most powerful of remedies—the therapy of compassion and love, the mercy of forgiveness, and the gift of enlightenment.

Hugo Enomiya-Lassalle makes a remarkable statement that, at first, appears far-fetched: "In the Mystical Age, the environment will self-correct." Enomiya-Lassalle, however, offers us a true vision. As the Mystical Age expands and pervades more and more of humanity, the environment will indeed correct itself, undergoing an "ecological remission." This will occur because a growing number of enlightened people (critical mass) will no longer rape and ravage the planet as has twentieth-century man *(the masculine gender is deliberately used here!)*. Great numbers of the human race will possess a sensitivity to the karmic results of thoughtless, destructive acts. As we sow, so shall we reap. Let us pray we may still forestall the whirlwind.

To repeat, there will be those the Mystical Age will leave behind in its evolutionary sweep, who will continue to act irresponsibly as before. Not all will be infused with higher consciousness—simply because of an unwillingness to make the effort and the sacrifices which the Mystical Age will demand of them. No one will participate in the Mystical Age without first making dedicated effort and life-simplifying sacrifices.

The Mystical Age will reveal the "hidden wholeness" of the cosmos, fantastically complicated, yet of a homogeneous oneness. It will proclaim anew the *shekinah* and mercy of our Motherly God. Otherwise, the world as we have known it may revert backwards, even perhaps to a time reminiscent of eons before Eden.

In the end, man destroyed the heaven that was called earth.
The earth had been beautiful until the spirit of man moved over it.
And man said "Let there be darkness." And there was darkness.

On the last day, there was a great noise over the face of the earth.
Fire consumed the beautiful globe, and there was ... silence.
The blackened earth now rested to worship the one true God.

And God saw all that man had done,
and in the silence over the smoldering ruins,
God wept.

—Reverse Creation (Anonymous)

8 ❧ A Divided Consciousness

We find ourselves divided between conscious and unconscious, psychological and physical, mind and matter. At the deepest level of consciousness, division disappears. All is one.

—Bede Griffiths, OSB[1]

The excessive, rationalistic bent of humanity is the product of a divided consciousness whereby the world is seen as an opaque "system of separateness," as a kind of "cosmic machine" made up of independent, disconnected pieces and parts. Other human beings become merely a "higher" type of separate "pieces" with whom we must deal. At the same time, we defend, sometimes violently, the "home turf" of our separate egocentric private selves.

All of the great religions have varying "theologies" of why humankind is so dysfunctional and in need of salvation from the illusory false self. Christianity proposes the myth (story) of the "fall," which, from that mysterious climactic event in prehistory, precipitated the "blinding of the intelligence and the weakening of the will" of all successive human beings. The story of Adam and Eve's expulsion from Eden is the story of the fall from unitive consciousness to divided consciousness, from oneness with all creation to separateness, confusion, and morbid self-reflection. It is signified by the sudden awareness of Adam and Eve that they were naked: "Then the eyes of both were opened, and they knew that they were naked; and they sewed fig leaves together and made loin-cloths for themselves" (Gen. 3:7).

Ever since, men and women have been plastering fig leaves over themselves, wrapping pleasures, money, and glory around themselves like bandages so as to make themselves appear successful, righteous, acceptable, desirable. It is the greatest and most enduring sham that has ever occurred in the cosmos! There are no lengths to which we will not go in order to cover up our nakedness. There is no end to the

masks we create for ourselves to disguise ourselves and keep the curious eyes of others from seeing who we really are. Yet all is illusion,
all is sham:

> There is no substance under the things with which I am clothed. I am
> hollow, and my structure of pleasures and ambitions has no foundation.
> I am objectified in them, but they are all destined by their very contin-
> gency to be destroyed. And when they are gone, there will be nothing
> left of me but my own nakedness and emptiness and hollowness, to tell
> me that I am my own mistake.
>
> —Thomas Merton[2]

At the same time it is important to understand that first man and
woman *had* to eat of the forbidden fruit of good and evil. It was a necessary evolutionary leap into a higher consciousness, the awakening
from an archaic consciousness, or a state of "preconsciousness," to
ego-consciousness, from raw instinct to a state of "knowing" whereby
early and future men and woman could *discriminate*. This new state
of consciousness, however, brought with it a heavy burden, a whole
package of undesirable realities that were to weigh heavily on the
back of humanity henceforth—sickness, suffering, a sense of alienation, and, most of all, the *angst* of living with his and her own private little separate consciousness.

Death was part of the package too. I believe those theologians are
correct who say that had there been no "fall" men and women would
have eventually died but would not have experienced death in the way
we presently experience it. It is speculated that, at some point, our
mortal bodies would have been assumed into heaven and there spiri-
tualized, without first undergoing earthly corruption. Otherwise a
quite sticky problem remains: there would now be *trillions* of people
crammed into this small spaceship earth!

One thing all the great religions agree on, although they may
understand and express it differently, is the need for "self-realization,"
for shedding the outer skin of the small ego-self.

> The creative and mysterious inner self must be delivered from the
> wasteful, hedonistic and destructive ego that seeks only to cover itself
> with disguises.
>
> —Thomas Merton[3]

So now we are back at square one. But the evolutionary dice are
rolling and, whatever number comes up, we can be sure it is more
than mere chance. The "house" is rolling the dice—and us along with
them—into the future, a future that will see the dismemberment of the
present ego-driven mental consciousness structure which has pro-
pelled humankind into the darkness of alienation:

> Reasoning and discrimination vanish after the attainment of God and
> communion with him. How long does a man reason and discriminate?
> As long as he is conscious of the manifold ... of "I" and "You." He
> becomes silent when he is truly aware of unity.
>
> —Sri Ramakrishna[4]

9 ❧ The Concentration Camp of Reason

We do not have time not to face what we are living in—a concentration camp of reason.

—Andrew Harvey[1]

Within the past fifteen or so years, the discovery by Robert Sperry that the human brain is bi-cameral, having left and right hemispheres, has itself greatly advanced the evolution of humankind. It is in the right brain where higher states of consciousness, like new stars, are birthed and evolve.

Western civilization is the product of an almost exclusively left-brain functioning, only rarely tapping its intuitive right-brain powers. Thus, we have become trapped in the "concentration camp" of reason, of analytical, pragmatic, and programmatic thinking. Only its geniuses, its artists, and its mystics have escaped left-brain confinement, revealing the splendor and awesome beauty which the intuitive, nonrational right brain is capable of birthing. One has only to listen to Mozart or Beethoven, to read the great poets, or to view the genius of a Michelangelo or a da Vinci to grasp the awesome potency of right-brain functioning. One has only to read the great mystics to understand that God communicates with us through the "intuitive spiritual faculties" of the right brain. Here is where the Sacred Feminine, the Divine Mother, communicates with us. It is here that the "cloud of unknowing" shields us from the diverting intrusions—and illusions—of ego-driven left-brain activities.

Virtually numberless are those in the West who live out their entire lives within the barbed wire fences of left-brain functioning. Rarely do they experience the joy and freedom which the Sacred Feminine offers us when we allow the right brain to be accessed under her delicate, gratuitous inspirations.

"Humankind," cried the great second-century Church Father

Irenaeus, "is potentiality for growth." Each of us is an infinite depth, rooted in the divine ground. Lying hidden within us is a treasure-trove of riches accessed via what the church fathers understood as our "spiritual faculties." These spiritual faculties are, in some myste-rious way, imbedded in the right hemisphere of the brain.

Origen was the first to have formulated the idea of five spiritual senses or faculties, corresponding to our five physical senses. This concept was subscribed to by many who followed him: Evagrius Ponticus, St. Basil the Great, St. Gregory of Nyssa, and Pseudo-Macarius, among others. It was further developed and commented upon by the twelfth-century doctor of the Church, St. Bonaventure. Origen states that "one can say that there exists, according to Scripture, a general sense or faculty for the divine." Origen would offer several characterizations of this "faculty for the divine," some-times referring to it as the "faculties of the interior man," "the facul-ties of the heart," "the spiritual senses," "a divine sensuality," "the powers of the soul." In our day, with the discovery that the brain is bi-cameral, I suggest that we can add: "the faculties of the right brain."

Origen's disciple, the fourth-century Egyptian Desert Father Evagrius Ponticus, states Origen's doctrine quite clearly and matter-of-factly: "The spirit possesses five spiritual senses which are means of perception and with which it fulfills the purpose of creation." Elsewhere he writes: "Just as every art demands a living faculty which is suitable for it, so the spirit as well needs a spiritual sense for the discernment of spiritual things."

Origen is emphatic in saying that just as our physical faculties are strengthened by constant practice, "it is the same with the spiritual senses ... where indeed a great deal of training is required." For Origen, this training is primarily a discipline of prayer/meditation: "Above all it is prayer which exercises the spiritual faculties. Everyone who trains himself in this way becomes one of the perfect." Origen speaks here of "contemplative" forms of prayer—prayer beyond words, images, ideas, and concepts. (See chapter "Right Meditation.")

Without the activation of our spiritual faculties, Origen insists, it is not possible to have "genuine mystical knowledge." Conversely, Origen states that "unbelief is shown precisely in the lack of the spiritual senses in certain people who are incapable of perceiving spiritual realities."

If our culture is to survive, the Mystical Age must permeate the very pores of Western society. Otherwise, Western culture as we know it, already largely soul-less, will continue to disintegrate and rot, hastening its demise by continuing to feed on the husks and fodder of the left-brain compost. A rich harvest is spread out before us, verdant fields of a great kingdom deep within us, which are accessed through our right-brain spiritual faculties. Truly, "the fields are white and ready for the harvest" (John 4:35).

The East has long been right-brain motivated and inspired, although without understanding it in such terms. It has been said— and correctly, I think—that the East has a contemplative piety that seems to be "built in" to their culture and history. The East, however, has little of the industriousness and energy of the West. Mystic Andrew Harvey recounts a conversation with a Tibetan master:

> Hundreds of people came to bring him presents but didn't stay to listen to his teaching. They wanted a blessing and nothing more. The same master said that if you can get Westerners to do spiritual work, they will do it with ardor and passion.

Andrew Harvey goes on to say:

> Westerners who have "easternized" their hearts and souls may be the most sophisticated beings that have ever been produced on the earth. They have developed all sorts of skills of discrimination that can then be very useful in the movement toward God.[2]

The West has made extraordinary strides and discoveries for the benefit of humanity in the areas of science, technology, its passion for justice and democracy and in realms of the physical world—areas largely ignored by the East. This is now changing. India's modern sage, Sri Aurobindo, insisted on the reality of the physical world and the need to deal with the great social and moral issues of our time. The Dalai Lama admits to the lack of social activism in Buddhism and has publicly stated this is an important lesson to be learned from Christianity.

As the confluence of the two great streams of East and West move closer and deeper, the possibility for a truly new global order of tolerance, harmony, and cooperation becomes no longer a Utopian dream but a real possibility. When the "right-brain East" and the "left-brain West" merge to reveal the wholeness and harmony of it all, then will unbridled left-brain thinking be relativized, propelling humankind over the barbed-wire fence of the concentration camp of reason.

> When number and numeral cease to be
> a power o'er the creaturely;
> When lovers, and the poets, far
> more learned than the scholars are;
> When world to free life can return,
> and to itself again adjourn;
> Where light and shade conjoin once more
> to the true clarity of yore;
> and tales of poetry provide
> to real-world history guide;
> Then can one cryptic word commence
> to drive the topsy-turvy hence.

—Novalis[3]

10   Owning Our Shadow

Who knows what evil lurks in the hearts of men? The Shadow knows!
—Intro., *The Shadow*, radio program

Before going beyond our whimsical opening quote, it should be made clear that what Carl Jung identifies as the "shadow" is not evil, but has the *potential to create evil* depending on how its hidden forces are dealt with. Jung understood the shadow as the receptacle of our personal unconscious, where all of our denied dark feelings, hostilities, unresolved conflicts, and negativities have been repressed and stored. When negative aspects of our personality come into view, it is the ego that instantly defends its "palace of perfection" from attack and hurls them "out of sight" deep into the unconscious.

In a showdown, God favors the shadow over the ego, for the shadow, with all its dangerousness, is closer to the center and more genuine.
—Robert A. Johnson[1]

It must be quickly said that the "shadow" is also the storehouse of latent noble and creative powers which, when they emerge, create poets, composers, artists, idealists, forces for good, even heroes.

Some of the pure gold of our personality is relegated to the shadow because it can find no place in that great levelling process that is culture. Our hero-worshipping capacity is pure shadow: our finest qualities are refused and laid on another. We often refuse to bear our noble truths and find a shadow substitute for them.
Robert A. Johnson[2]

"Heaven and skid row," writes Jungian analyst Robert A. Johnson, "are separated only by an act of consciousness." To make life-enhancing acts of consciousness we must be in touch with our shadow, accepting what is hidden there as part of ourselves. When the recognition of our inferior characteristics threatens to smear our carefully air-brushed self-portrait, we are quickly wont to say to ourselves: "That's not me. I'm certainly not that kind of person!"

It is never our conscious mind that projects our shadow onto others, but our unconscious. We do not activate the shadow—it just happens, suddenly and without warning. When "shadow material" enters our consciousness, it always carries with it an emotional charge, great or small, which is the first indication that the shadow is unloading a portion of its content.

This emotional charge is the "red flag" (red = color of emotion) we must learn to recognize and quickly, properly respond to before it can inflict damage, before the shadow can project its negativity onto others. At the same time, we need the energies of the shadow to act the way we properly should. It is a matter of directing the shadow energies, not letting them direct us.

We own our shadow when we recognize and accept these negative, inferior aspects of our personality as being part of who we really are rather than some phantasm that flies into our consciousness. Instead of repressing (denying) these sudden "revelations of truth," we must accept them as part and parcel of who we are, a part that needs release and healing. This is usually done by calmly staying with these uncomfortable, disconcerting emotional charges and giving them a chance to unload.

Those who can calmly, prayerfully do this—placing these irruptions in God's hands when they surface for the length of time they remain— will find that the "Divine Therapist" will heal the great majority of these unresolved conflicts. Those which sometimes may be violent and powerful will return again if not vented the first time. Such more violent irruptions of the shadow may call for speaking with an understanding friend to help us "work through" the conflict. Or it may sometimes require the help of a professional therapist. This process of unloading requires patience and the courage to admit to ourselves that we are not as wonderful and perfect as the self-portrait we continually "touch up" and paint of ourselves.

The "collective unconscious" of a nation can spew out its shadow on another country, spawning wars and mass suffering. Hitler's shadow, bought into by millions of his followers—which thereby became the *nation's* collective shadow—thrust the world into a devastating global war and caused the untold suffering of millions of innocents.

Thomas Merton, recognizing and owning his shadow, has written that in another time, in another place, he could have been a Nazi guard at Auschwitz. St. Theresa of Lisieux, who was aware that God had made her a saint (with her heroic cooperation!) wrote that, had she not become a saint, she could have become one of the most evil people on earth! Thus, we can be saints or devils. Gold and darkness both await discovery and release in our shadow.

It is often tragic to see how blatantly a man bungles his own life and the lives of others, yet remains totally incapable of seeing how much the whole tragedy originates in himself, and how he continuously feeds it and keeps it going. It is an unconscious factor that spins the illusions that veil his world.

—Carl Jung[3]

Owning our shadow and allowing it to dissipate in a calm, patient way, rather than projecting it on those around us, can be likened perhaps to taking our garbage to the landfill rather than scattering it all over town by blowing it up with dynamite! Alcoholics Anonymous has devised something called a "God bag," a small receptacle in which a person writes down the immediate problem he or she may be facing and unable to resolve, and places the scrap of paper in the "God bag," asking God, after they have done their best, to take care of the problem. It may sound trite, but there is overwhelming evidence that it works in a great number of cases.

What has this to do with the new consciousness? When the Sacred Feminine is rediscovered and accessed, her grace and wisdom will give us the courage to touch (observe) and own (accept) our repressed shadow material as it emerges "piece by piece." In the process of owning our shadow, we become gradually healed, become more whole and individuated. We become more truly human.

To honor and accept one's own shadow is a profound religious discipline. It is whole-making and thus holy and the most important experience of a lifetime.

—Robert A. Johnson[4]

Part Two
The Sacred Feminine

If the new consciousness is to rise within humanity like the leaven of new yeast, it must emerge from the womb of the Sacred Feminine. Humanity must be born again not only "from above" but also "from within" if it is to survive even the next fifty years.

Unless the aggressive masculine powers are integrated with the feminine powers of gentleness, compassion, intuition, love of nature, and the like, then our planet—like the out-of-orbit asteroid which recently crashed into Jupiter—will continue to career out of control, destined for destruction.

This is to say that humanity must begin, and quickly, to access the powers of the feminine, already innate within the race, to offset and counterbalance the aggressive masculine energies that have almost exclusively dictated the course of Western history over the past centuries.

It is important that we better understand, specifically and concretely, what is meant when we say that humanity must receive from the Sacred Feminine the gifts that only she can offer us, the gifts that alone can save us from a death wish that is close to being fulfilled.

11 🌿 Hagia Sophia

There is in all visible things an invisible fecundity, a dimmed light, a meek namelessness, a hidden wholeness. This mysterious unity and integrity is Wisdom, the Mother of all. It rises up in wordless gentleness and flows out to me from the unseen roots of all created being, welcoming me tenderly, saluting me with indescribable humility. This is at once my own being, my own nature, and the Gift of my Creator's Thought and Art within me, speaking as Hagia Sophia, speaking as my sister, Wisdom.

—Thomas Merton[1]

In one of his most masterful poetic prose writings, Merton goes on to write:

The feminine principle in the world is the inexhaustible source of creative realizations of the Father's glory. She is his manifestation in radiant splendor! But she remains unseen, glimpsed by only a few.[2]

The poem declares that Hagia Sophia, *Holy Wisdom*, is in all things and is the Divine Life reflected in them … the love by which the Divine is "outpoured" into us and the love that enfolds us.

It would be a great mistake and a futile undertaking to try to define precisely and to circumscribe the Sacred Feminine in words, for she is beyond all thought and transcends all pragmatic and objective investigation. She is in all, sustains and nurtures all, but does so "hiddenly." She is the mystery of life, a life that must not and cannot be analyzed out into Cartesian finalities, but must be lived trustingly and spontaneously. She is Wisdom. If we try to analyze her mystery, we will only fall back into the pit out of which we are trying to climb. Life should not be conducted like a business. Life should flow like poetry.

Hagia Sophia is the Mother who is to be found in the spirituality of the Native American and the Aborigine, who revere her as Mother

43

Earth and Sky, in fire and water, in the plants and seedlings. She "gifts" them with food and drink, nurtures them with milk from her breasts, and endows them with a primordial wisdom that the "great civilizations" of our time have forgotten, have buried beneath an avalanche of greed and lust for power.

It is the myths (stories) and symbols of primitive, tribal peoples that have always been seen as ways to free humankind from their isolation and separation from nature, and restore people to unity with themselves and with the universe. It is precisely this unitive-holistic vision which modern "civilized" men and women most need to recover. This ancient vision of a cosmos sustained by an all-pervading Spirit is what we in the West must learn from the East, and from tribal peoples everywhere.

> I would go so far as to say that if we do not listen with respect and humility to what the Kogis, Native Americans, Bushmen, Ladakhis and Aborigines have to tell us, we will not survive. These prophetic traditions arise out of a relationship with nature at once more visionary and more rooted than ours, and they warn us with a passion, an urgency, a dignity and quite extraordinary accuracy of what will happen if we continue to disobey.
>
> —Andrew Harvey[3]

The great religions of the world have largely forgotten her and, in so doing, they have incurred self-inflicted wounds in dire need of the Mother's healing therapy. Religion itself needs to be born again, as indeed it will be as the Mystical Age moves relentlessly forward.

In the Gospel of John, Nicodemus—misunderstanding the words of Jesus about being born again—witlessly asks the question: "How can one go back into his mother's womb?" For us, for humanity, *it is the only way back to Eden!* We must return to our Mother's womb and be born again out of her love and tenderness and compassion and wisdom. There is no other way. Otherwise, we will remain spiritual midgets, continuing to grasp at everything we deceptively think will assuage the *angst* that festers within our collective bowels.

Meditating on Merton's poem, one sees clearly that our hope, our salvation, our highest aspirations—indeed, our future as a race—depend on our returning to the womb of the Mother, Holy Wisdom, to relearn what once she taught us but we long ago forgot. Like spoiled children, we have run off on our own egocentric folly-trip, have forgotten her teachings, and have wound up wondering how ever did we get in such an *ungodly* mess!

As we look about us and see the evil, suffering, and destruction we ourselves have created, we must not—we cannot—succumb to despair and hopelessness. The love and tender mercy of the Mother are without bounds, infinitely deep in their compassion and love for us. But we must respond and act quickly. We are living on borrowed time. Our planet is dying, and if our planet dies, we die with it.

Return we must to the Mother's womb.

God is at once Father and Mother. As Father he stands in solitary might surrounded by darkness. As Mother, his shining is diffused, embracing all his creatures with merciful tenderness and light. The Diffuse Shining of God is Hagia Sophia. We call her his "glory." In Sophia, his power is experienced only as mercy and as love.

—Thomas Merton[4]

12 🌿 Death of a Mystic

> I felt that the right brain, the earth, the feminine, came and hit me. What I understood later was that the left brain, the whole rational system, had been knocked down and the intuitive understanding had been opened up. It's gone on ever since. The left brain continues to work, but the right brain is in control.
>
> —Bede Griffiths[1]

Early on the morning of January 25, 1990, while Bede Griffiths was meditating in his Shantivanam ashram in southern India, he was suddenly struck by a terrific force—"like a sledgehammer," as he later described it. This force seemed to be dragging him out of his chair. He was able to crawl into bed, where he did not move or speak for a week, a period of which he later had no memory. He awoke one night and expected to die, as others in the ashram also thought. He waited to die, but nothing happened. Suddenly a "voice" came to him and said: "Surrender to the Mother." That was all—"Surrender to the Mother."

Fr. Bede later recounted how, immediately after hearing the voice, he experienced tremendous love, recalling: "waves of love flooded over me." He even called out to a nearby friend: "I am being overwhelmed by love!" The "Black Madonna" came into his consciousness, the mother of earth and the heavens, but also motherhood as a whole. "It was very violent at first, but then it became very loving—and it has gone on ever since."

From that moment on, he experienced a profound sense of *advaita* (nonduality):

> All division broke down and everything was flowing into everything else.... Today I see the divisions of people and things as different, but, at the same time, it is all one. I have never lost that sense of all diversity contained in the one.

46

This experience of *advaita* gave Bede Griffiths a clearer insight into the mystery of the Trinity. In one of the most penetrating and beautiful allusions to the Three Persons in the unity of One Divinity, he spontaneously whispered:

> The Father is the Ground, beyond name and form, and from the One comes his self-expression, the Word that expresses the Father. From this union of relationship with the Father, the source of being, the origin, the abyss of being, the emptiness, the darkness, comes forth the Word, the Wisdom and Light.
>
> The Son reveals the Father, the abyss, and manifests all that is latent in the Godhead, all the seeds of creation. And in the Son the seeds come to life and the whole of creation is mirrored in the Son, all time and space, and you and I–all is already present in that one Reality. All the "ideas" in the Word come into being through the Spirit, the shakti, the energy, the divine power–and that is what propels the whole universe.

The "Big Bang," he went on to say, was in the Word, and became manifest through the Spirit, and then came out into time and space (time/space occurring simultaneously).

Over the remaining three years of his life, Fr. Bede would proclaim that it is the Mother who is the womb of evolving creation, and that the power and grace of the Mother are now being poured out upon the planet and its inhabitants in a new and dynamic way. The Divine Feminine is coming to heal the great rift in the world, coming to temper its excessive patriarchal bias, often manifested as mindless exploitation, rigid authoritarianism, and repressive control. The *anima* is being integrated with the *animus*. Until now, the collective aggressive masculine powers of the *animus* have succeeded in pushing the world off its axis. If we imagine our planet to be a player in a cosmic pinball game, we are dangerously close to triggering: *TILT–GAME OVER!*

On his ashram deathbed in 1993 Fr. Bede spoke these words: "The hour of God and mankind's greatest ordeal is now here." Asked if we would be able to survive, he answered:

> The mercy and the help of God is always stretched out to us, always. Even now at this late hour. But we must be humble enough to ask for

them. Everything depends on whether we can abandon our pride before it is too late.[2]

A few months before he returned to India to die, I had the grace and privilege of speaking with him in San Francisco. Hearing that he was to give a talk there, I impetuously hopped on a plane to the coast, sensing that he had only a short time left on this earth. I shall always remember this gaunt, ascetic-looking Sannyasin, whose radiant appearance communicated something incommunicable. In his "River of Compassion," Bede Griffiths penned these words from the Vedas:

> I am the Father of the universe. I am the Mother of the universe, and the creator of all. I am the highest to be known, the path of purification, the holy OM, the Three Vedas.[3]

13 🌿 The Mother

To the property of motherhood belong nature, love, wisdom and knowledge, and this is God. I it am. The greatness and goodness of the Father,
I it am. The wisdom and kindness of the Mother, I it am. The light and
grace that is all blessed love, I it am.

—Julian of Norwich[1]

The Sacred Feminine ... Hagia Sophia ... the Sacred Divine ... the
Mother—all are names for the same Reality, a Reality we call God,
Allah, Atman, Yahweh, Great Spirit. When Bede Griffiths lay dying, he
would be asked, "What is the Mother to you now?" He would always
smile and say: "There are no words for her."

Although there are "no words for her," no definitions possible, no
theological statements that would diminish and confine her, Andrew
Harvey has given us an insight into the "Divine Motherliness":

> The experience of the Mother, of the mother-aspect of the Godhead, of
> the Motherhood of God, is an immense, vast, constantly expanding
> experience of the presence of calm and blissful unconditional love as
> the ground of all being.
>
> Everything is in the Mother ... the Mother is beyond everything,
> constantly drawing everything deeper and deeper in the fire of her
> always transforming love. She is at once the ground, the energy and the
> always changing and flowering goal of evolution.[2]

Andrew Harvey goes on to say that while the Mother cannot be
grasped by the mind, she can be known in a deep mystical experience.
Although not a Catholic, he points out that "in the past 150 years or
so, the Virgin Mary has been appearing with astonishing regularity
all around the world. The Church has been extremely slow to recognize ... the passionate urgency of her messages to humankind."[3] He
notes that the Trinity has almost always been considered "masculine."
"Until the sacred feminine is invited into every aspect of the
Trinity ... until the mystics are brought into the core of the Church's

teaching, Christianity can never recover its sacred transforming force."[4]

It is not Catholicism alone that must recover the Sacred Feminine. Neither Islam, Hinduism, Judaism, or Buddhism has developed a vision of the Mother, though they must if they are to join the mutation to higher-consciousness. Andrew Harvey makes the following observation on the thought of Sri Aurobindo:

> To this immense awareness of the many-sided glory of the Mother, Aurobindo added one essential and revolutionary ingredient; a vision of the Mother, the Shakti, as the force that powers the evolution of the universe and as the force that would sustain, encourage and create the next stage in the evolutionary development of humankind. He realized the Mother as the architect of evolution, the summoner of humanity to a supreme and endless adventure of self-transformation.
>
> —Andrew Harvey[5]

The light and grace of the Mother have already "descended" upon our broken world. If we are sufficiently humble, grateful, and courageous in our determination to follow her inspirations, then we too will be the heralds of a new evolutionary uplifting of the race. The Mystical Age will truly be *our* age, an age resplendent and richly endowed. If we will but take her hand, a hand now mercifully outstretched to us, we can become her emissaries, transducers of her light to those near and around us and beyond into the future.

> Through her representatives on earth at the moment, the Divine Mother is showing the world that normal life is compatible with supreme realization, and that direct mystical contact with the Divine can be sustained in any activity or setting.
>
> A new spiritual age has dawned . . . an age in which the Divine will be present intimately, normally, consciously in all things and activities in which the Divine life . . . will be lived normally on earth.
>
> —Andrew Harvey[6]

14 ❧ Womb of Our Rebirth

They asked the Rabbi of Lubin:
Why is it that in the holy Book of Splendor,
the turning to God is called "Mother"?

He explained: "When a man confesses and
repents, when his heart accepts understanding,
he becomes like a newborn child, and
his own turning to God is his mother."
                                —Martin Buber[1]

The womb of the Mother we must enter to be re-created is the cave of our own heart, the birthing ground of new being. Here the Mother waits to bless us with her gifts. Thus, we do not have to travel far to enter the primordial womb-darkness of the Sacred Feminine, though the journey is sometimes difficult and not without risks.

We must also refuse to remain on the exhausting treadmill of useless activity and mundane pursuits that sap our vital energies and waste our gifts and talents on empty and foolish things. We must detach ourselves from the allurements and attractions of the world which keep us scattered, in which there is only death, and which prevent us from hearing her voice and her inspirations over the din of the day. *We cannot become detached from the world until we become detached from ourselves,* from our false ego-self.

We must draw back from the clutter and confusion of the world whenever such opportunity is offered us, stringing together golden moments of quiet reflection and wordless recollection. Otherwise, how shall we learn to cleave to God if all our energies of mind and spirit are constantly bound over hand and foot in the service of Mammon—a capitulation to illusion that bleeds our powers, carrying them downstream on a river of the blood of others? How shall we learn compassion, the great fruit of love, if we don't give ourselves

51

the silence to grow and, like the leafy branches of a tree, to then reach out and give others shade and comfort?

> You must enter the solitude of prayer with the conviction that, in finding God, you will find a greater love for your brothers. God draws those he loves into solitude until they are fully formed. Every person needs solitude to find and develop himself. Otherwise he will remain a child. He will be afraid of being left alone, face to face with himself. And if the Christian cannot live alone, face to face with his God, then the Church is only an immense herd and is no longer the Church of Christ.
>
> —Yves Raguin[2]

We are nothing without compassion. With the practice of compassion—the way of self-giving and solicitude for others and all living beings—we hew out a "shortcut" to enlightenment. In the process of self-giving, we empty ourselves of our shallowness and falsity and prepare the soil of our hearts for the seeds of contemplation. The Christian must keep in mind that the greatest purifying asceticism is the practice of the Christian virtues; for the Buddhist, dedication to the Eightfold Path. Such spiritually motivated action cuts deeply into the ego, clearing away the dead fatty tissue of selfishness that thwarts the free flow of the Spirit. Teilhard de Chardin reminds us that "the only climate in which we can continue to grow is that of devotion and self-denial in a spirit of brotherhood."

An "engaged love" such as this is gifted us from the Divine Mother, an ever-deepening, ever-widening process of inner growth. Jesus commanded that his disciples must love one another as he loved them. But this is a command impossible to obey—until we grow and are gifted in his love, the Christ-love poured into us by the indwelling Spirit (Gal. 4:6).

John A. Sanford, an Episcopalian priest and Jungian psychologist, brings this clearly home to us in his book *Mystical Christianity*. Turning to the original Greek of the last chapter of the Gospel of John, Sanford points out that the word for "love" is expressed several different ways in Greek, the original language of the Christian scriptures. When Jesus asks Peter three times "Do you love me?" the Lord uses the word *agapaō* the first two times he addresses Peter. Peter, in responding, employs a *lesser* word—*phileō*—to proclaim his love, a word more akin to "deep affection." It would seem that Peter is painfully aware he is not capable of loving Jesus with the same intense love that Jesus has for him. He qualifies his response, using the word *phileō* instead of *agapaō*. Then an amazing thing happens–impossible to grasp from our English translations. The third time Jesus queries Peter, he comes down to Peter's level, seeing that Peter is not yet capable of *agape*-love, Jesus now uses Peter's word, *phileō*. Peter answers for the third time with the same word, *phileō*. In our imagination, we can envision Peter figuratively "wiping his brow" in relief–knowing he no longer is being asked to meet Jesus on the much deeper ground of *agapaō*.[3]

The Christian is called to be God-like, a process that the Eastern fathers call *divinization*–to become perfect in selfless love as our heavenly Father/Mother is perfect. If this was beyond our capacity, it would not be demanded of us. It is primarily God's work, not ours, except for our cooperation. As Augustine wrote: "God did not ask your permission when he created you. He will not sanctify you without it!"

Just as Christ "emptied himself of his divinity and took the form of a slave" (Phil. 2:6-7) so too must we be emptied. Enomiya-Lassalle remarks that the prerequisite for enlightenment, for contemplation, for radical transformation of consciousness, is *emptiness*–what the Greek fathers called *kenōsis*. The Buddhist declares that emptiness (*sunyata*) is the prerequisite for enlightenment. We must become *kenotic Christians*, people emptied of worldly attachments, self-absorption constantly dealing with our "pimply little selves." This is a matter of being freed from illusion; from clinging to falsity; from grasping at the hollow, the mundane, the transient, and the trivial. It is a matter of being freed from an ego that feeds on illusion and is nurtured by the lies of society and the world. Commenting on this as it is treated in the great spiritual paths of the East, Thomas Merton writes:

> In all these higher religious traditions the path to transcendent real-ization (enlightenment) is a path of ascetic self-emptying and "self-naughting," and not at all a path of self-affirmation, or self-fulfillment.[4]

This, in society's view, is foolishness and insanity. The cleansing, purifying process of *kenōsis* is the work of grace. Our part is to keep our hearts open to receive and cooperate with the gratuitous healing love-therapy of our Divine Mother. To open ourselves to her benevolence, we must descend into the "womb of our hearts" and, in silence, in solitude, and in faith, await and confidently expect her secret transforming action upon the deepest recesses of our being.

If our hearts, re-created, are pure, then, as the sixth beatitude promises (Matt. 5:8), we shall "see" God, in "luminous obscurity." We shall "see" in proportion as our hearts have been purified. Only the impurities of our hearts prevent the "Taboric Light" from shining upon our consciousness and breaking through the dense shroud of our little shriveled-up private selves.

15 ❧ The Mystic and the Sacred Feminine

Mystics must be returned to full glory to the world. Without them, humanity is a desolate orphan.

—Andrew Harvey[1]

Someone whose words I trust told me the story of a friend, a Hindu mystic, who had a private audience with John Paul II. The Pope, who is very worried about the state of the Church, asked him for advice as to what he might do. The Hindu mystic replied: "Gather in your mystics!"

Every realized mystic, of whatever spiritual tradition, has "touched" the Sacred Feminine and has integrated the *anima* and *animus* powers into their total personality. Until this integration occurs, no one—regardless of how disciplined one's ascetic practices—can become a mystic, a "container" of Truth. The Christian mystic experiences Truth as "Christ consciousness," the experience that "in Him we live and breathe and have our being" (Acts 17:28).

The non-Christian mystic experiences Truth differently—some impersonally, as does the Buddhist; others personally, as do the Sufi mystics, the Jewish mystics, and those who follow certain forms of Hinduism, especially the Bhakti devotional path. Truth reveals herself differently according to one's personal history, culture, indoctrination, and foundational teachings. Like different shafts of light of a prism, the "prism of truth" radiates in different hues, shades, and colors. Every true mystic could pen these identical words yet experience them differently:

> Sitting in meditation on my carpet,
> I have seen the Supreme being,
> bathed in the Light that is beyond all light.
> Less than the smallest grain,
> greater than all greatness,
> is He—

Him I have found beyond the reaches of sense,
piercing the veil of my body.
                                    —Tagore, The Dying Year

Undeniably, there are "varieties of mystical experience" (cf. William James) that are real and transformative, each shot through and through with the grace and wisdom of the Sacred Feminine. Ultimately, the Sacred Feminine cannot be "named" or defined, even by the most skilled theology. She is Mystery and is always experienced as such—transcendent beyond all finalities, yet immanent in her revelation—closer to us than we are to ourselves. She is *sunyata*, emptiness, yet inexplicable fullness. She is the immense abyss of darkness that is also the creating womb of light, love, and wisdom. She is love, that enfolds, permeates, and vivifies the cosmos, enshrouding it with mercy, compassion, and loving kindness.

The mystic "knows" with greater certitude than the scientist or the theologian or the philosopher. Mystics hold Truth within themselves and are living containers of the real, the eternal. Mystics are in possession of Truth because Truth possesses *them*. The Sacred/Divine Feminine is latent and immanent within us all, waiting to be discovered—the pearl of great price hidden in the deepest ground of our unconscious. The discovery of her is not so much the consequence of our own efforts, however dedicated, but more the unpredictable gratuitous "implosion" of her reality into our consciousness, providing we have prepared for her arrival.

Carl Jung declared that there could be no mystical union with God without accessing the feminine powers of the *anima* and integrating them with the masculine powers of the *animus:*

> If the individuation process is made conscious, consciousness must confront the unconscious and a balance between the opposites must be found. The religious need longs for wholeness, and therefore lays hold of the images of wholeness offered by the unconscious ... which rise up from the unconscious.[2]

Until the feminine powers of intuition, sensitivity, gentleness, compassion, receptivity, and reverence for nature are "married" with the masculine *animus* energies of will, drive, passion for order and control, genuine mystical experience will remain unrealized. This "sacred marriage" heals the "split" within our psyche and re-creates us whole. (See chapter "Wedding Bells.") Individuation is not holiness. Nonetheless, it is a prerequisite for accessing the deeper realms of the psyche which, like the lotus flower, has the "energy" to open out into the mystical state. In Christianity, it is called infused contemplation.

We must first, however, "pull ourselves together" and become, in Jung's term, individuated. We must cease being continually scattered of mind and dispersed in our actions. We must develop some meaningful degree of unity if the lotus flower within is to gradually open wide her petals.

> The first thing you have to do before you start thinking about such a thing as contemplation is to try to recover your basic natural unity, to reintegrate your compartmentalized being into a coordinated and simple whole, and learn to live as a unified person. This means that you have to bring back together the fragments of your distracted existence so that when you say "I" there is someone really present to support the pronoun you have uttered.
>
> —Thomas Merton[3]

The great fourteenth-century mystic Meister Eckhart expressed the archetypal symbol of the feminine dwelling within us in these daring words:

> For man to become fruitful, he must become a woman. Woman! That is the most noble word that can be addressed to the soul. That man should conceive God within himself is good ... but that God should become fruitful in him is better. For to become fruitful through the gift received is to be grateful for the gift. And then the intellect becomes a woman in its gratitude and conceives anew.[4]

16 ❧ The Souls of Our Children

Suffer the little children to come to me, for it is to such as these that the Kingdom of Heaven belongs.

—Mark 10:14–15

If I were to interpret these words of Jesus allegorically, I would suggest that Jesus is saying: "Quickly, bring the children to me, and protect them from worldly society, for there their very souls will be in jeopardy."

Growing up in today's America, our children hardly have a chance to evolve spiritually; they are never given the opportunity and the nurturing environment to develop their uniqueness and their special innate qualities and potential. Children possess a natural capacity for "spiritual rearing" and education—even for meditation, if only they can be reached in time.

Thich Nhat Hanh tells the story of a four-year-old boy who came with his mother to one of his Zendo retreats. He offered to teach the young boy meditation, but his mother objected, saying "like all boys that age" he would not be able to sit still in meditation. Thich Nhat Hanh asked her how long she thought her child could sit in silence and stillness. "About four seconds," his mother replied. She agreed, however, to allow the great teacher to "try his best." The mother went on about other things, later asking him: "How long did my son sit in meditation?" "Forty minutes," replied Hanh.

Between a society that long ago lost its sacred view of life and an obsolete educational system, our children have their life-essence squeezed out of them before reaching the age of puberty. They are the innocent and unfortunate victims of a culture of rationalism and materialism that threatens to drain their very soul-blood, a culture that promotes competition but not compassion, individualism but not personalism, knowledge but not wisdom. Our schools are incapable of educating *the whole person*, only those aspects of the human potential that are "marketable." We eradicate what is most precious and vital in our young. If you wish an example of mediocrity, then look to the American educational system. Today America spends some five hundred billion dollars on education, yet there has been no improvement in reading and other basic skills since decades ago when only twenty-three billion dollars was spent on "educating" our youth.

In one of his rare scathing utterances, Jesus warned: "Whosoever scandalizes one of these little ones, it would be better for him that a millstone be placed around his neck and he be cast into the sea" (Matt. 18:6). Western society is inflicting more than scandal on its little ones—it is polluting their souls. When that inevitable "someday" arrives when we are called to "own up," the only thing we will be able to plead is—ignorance.

One cannot escape the implication that children held a special place in the heart and concern of the Galilean, nor escape the implied admonition that we have a special responsibility to nurture their journey into adulthood. "Everything is prefigured in the child," said the sixteenth-century Swiss physician and alchemist Percelsus, "it must only be awakened and summoned forth."

Two friends of mine have developed a vision that bears the title of this chapter, "The Souls of Our Children." The following is from the program prospectus:

> The Souls of our Children focuses on the spiritual lives of children and teen-agers. Our mission is to heal the spiritual trauma of young people and help guide them onto their own path to spiritual wholeness and maturity.
>
> The future of our planet lies deep within the souls of our children. This program developed out of our work with the special education of young people and a new model for understanding and cultivating youth spirituality. We approach spirituality as the "embodied awareness of sacred interconnectedness" and believe it is a basic need, drive and intelligence. Our strategy is research, education and advocacy through a framework of community-building.
>
> We are hopeful that through dissemination of educational materials and programs, networking, and media work, we plan on making the spiritual life of young people a national issue. We believe that spiritual neglect is as devastating as any other form of neglect and that the spiritual lives of young people is a major issue.

The "Souls of Our Children" program, in which I have been asked to participate, is a program awaiting funding and the support of like-minded advocates. In enterprises such as this lie the hope of our children and the salvation of the race. Such a vision, once integrated into the new mutation of consciousness, will bring about sweeping and enduring changes and enormous benefits to the human family.

It is my opinion that when man has integrated the fourth dimension—that is, when children reach the fourth dimension in the same matter-of-fact way that they now attain to rational thinking at a certain age—humanity will have achieved enlightenment.

—Enomiya-Lassalle[1]

17 ℞ Experiment in the Ever-Present Future

The first principle of true teaching is that nothing can be taught. The
teacher . . . is only a helper and a guide. His business is to suggest and
not to impose. The second principle is that the mind has to be con-
sulted in its own growth. The idea of hammering a child into the shape
desired by the parent or teacher is a barbarous and ignorant supersti-
tion. The third principle is to work from the near to the far, from that
which is to that which shall be. The past is our foundation, the present
our material, the future our aim and summit.

—Sri Aurobindo[1]

There is a place on this tortured planet where a great and noble
experiment is being successfully carried out that honors and nurtures
the souls of our children and honors the Sacred Feminine. It is a
vision that has been actualized since its founding in 1968, a community stretching out to its goal of working and living together in community in a special way, integrating the new consciousness. This
special place is called Auroville, in southern India, where work, education, silence, stillness, and meditation are the fabric of community
life, fostering openness and receptivity to the grace and inspirations
of the Divine Mother. It was founded by Sri Aurobindo's "spiritual col-
laborator," an Algerian-born, former French nationalist, Mira Richard,
who was to become known simply as "the Mother." She lived some
twenty years after Sri Aurobindo's death in 1950. (Aurobindo would
say of her: "The mother's consciousness and mine are the same.") The
idea and schema of Auroville are based on the writings of Aurobindo
(*The Human Cycle* [1918]), and it may be described as a community
practicing "the science of living."

"One lives in Auroville," wrote its foundress, "in order to be free of
moral and social convention. But this liberty must not be a new slav-
ery to the ego, its desires and its ambitions." As described by Robert
McDermott, the translator and editor of many of Aurobindo's volu-
minous writings:

Auroville is a place where all human beings of good will, sincere in their aspirations, could live freely as citizens of the world . . . a place of peace, concord, harmony, where all the fighting instincts of man would be used exclusively to conquer the causes of suffering and misery, to surmount his weaknesses and ignorance, to triumph over his limitations and incapacities; a place where the needs of the spirit would take precedence over the satisfaction of desires and passions and the seeking for material pleasures and enjoyment.[2]

Many years before Auroville was created, the poet-educator Rabindranath Tagore seemed to yearn for such a place, when from America in 1921 he wrote:

I want just a small place where I shall try to build up a community of men and women who will recognize no geographical boundaries. They will know only one country and that country will comprise the entire human race.

Tagore would later further explain his aims and dream:

I have tried to develop in the children of my school the freshness of their feeling for Nature, a sensitiveness of soul in their relationship with their human surroundings.[3]

There is an adage and teaching in Auroville . . .

No one ought to speak of the Divine unless he or she has had experience of the Divine. It is only in experience that one can have knowledge of the Divine. Get experience of the Divine—then only will you have the right to speak of it.

Would that all the "God-talk" that flutters about so casually be so experientially grounded—without which all such talk rings hollow, and which trivializes true religion. It is neither helpful nor fruitful to talk much about God. One who has been truly touched by God is brought to a deep interior silence, to a "secret" one cannot express, nor does one wish to.

Education in Auroville is regarded not with the view of passing exams or out-performing one's neighbor, but for "enriching the existing faculties" in children and "bringing forth new ones." All forms of the creative arts are fostered and encouraged. Social status is refused a foothold, and work is looked upon not simply as a means of livelihood but as a way of expressing oneself and developing innate capacities and possibilities.

The requirements for becoming part of the community of Auroville are set forth in the Auroville Charter:

> Auroville belongs to nobody in particular. Auroville belongs to humanity as a whole. But to live in Auroville one must be a willing servitor of the Divine Consciousness.
>
> Auroville will be the place of an unending education, of constant progress, and a youth that never ages.
>
> Auroville wants to be the bridge between the past and the future, taking advantage of all discoveries from without and from within; Auroville will boldly spring towards future realizations.
>
> Auroville will be the site of material and spiritual researches for a living embodiment of an actual Human Unity.[4]

Those who have visited Auroville and remained for a while report that the spirit of Auroville (the spirit of Sri Aurobindo) is substantially but not entirely alive and well. History has shown that the farther we get from the founders, the more their vision becomes diluted. "Aurovillians" understand, however, the reality of the times and see their experiment as exactly that, an experiment–but one that some day will, it is hoped, "take fire" as the new consciousness expands and becomes integrated.

The question remains: Of what practical use is Auroville for the rest of us, for humanity in general? First, there needs to be a physical place on planet earth where the new consciousness is being fully integrated *in community*–a "living experiment" in the ever-present future. Second, by observing Auroville, we might learn about how to apply various ethical values, some of which we may be able to presently integrate into select areas of human society.

Perhaps there are existing educational models in the West that have broken out of the prevailing obsolete educational structure and may be fertile ground for some of the ideas and values being lived out in Auroville. Perhaps a study of Auroville might inspire the creation of similar communities in the West, where they are most needed.

In the final analysis, the new-consciousness model of Auroville must be implemented and integrated *in the home*, by adult family members who are themselves "citizens of the fourth spiritual dimen-

sion." This means people who are not so much "religious" as deeply
spiritual, who are mystics and have transcended dogma and doctrine
and are living experientially and integratively the truths that dog-
matic statements can, at best, only point to.

> The earth is not ready to realize such an idea (as Auroville), for
> mankind does not yet possess the necessary knowledge to understand
> or accept it, nor the indispensable consciousness to enforce it. That is
> why I call it a "dream" ... but a dream that is on the way to becoming
> a reality. That is what we are seeking to do at the Ashram of Sri
> Aurobindo on a small scale. The achievement is indeed far from perfect,
> but it is progressive; little by little we advance towards our goal.
>
> —The Mother[5]

Part Three
Characteristics of the
New Consciousness

❦ The future-at-hand is not predictable in terms of specific events and occurrences that will later define it—no more than the Axial Age could have been defined at its outset approximately twenty-five hundred years ago. Even the general assignment of dates is impossible.

Nonetheless, we shall need evidence that the new consciousness is indeed taking shape and being integrated into humanity—if only to sustain our hope that we will survive the gathering storm. We must look first to the source of our present difficulties—Western culture. If the new mutation does not occur here, and soon, then we should prepare for the very worst.

Like a painter who first faces a blank canvas, the details and particulars of the final painting emerge by degrees as the artist continues to work and the defining brush strokes gradually complete the painting.

18 ❧ Recovery of the Sacred

> There was a time when meadow, grove and stream
> and every common sight did seem to me
> apparelled in celestial light,
> the glory and the freshness of a dream.
>
> It is not now as it has been of yore.
> Turn where so'er I may by night or day
> The things which I have seen
> I now can see no more.
>
> Our birth is but a sleep and a forgetting.
> The soul that rises with us, our life's star
> hath had elsewhere its setting
> and cometh from afar
> not in entire forgetfulness
> and not in utter nakedness
> but trailing clouds of glory do we come
> from God who is our home.
>
> —William Wordsworth, "Prelude"

There was a time, until the high Middle Ages, when the West (Europe) held dear a sacred view of life, which was the "gyroscope" that kept people upright and the "ballast" that kept people grounded in reality. The "pearl of great price" was once our treasure, the holy aspirations and deep yearnings of our hearts, its sparkling crown. Then, in haughty arrogance, we began to look to other gods called "reason" and "progress" and imagined we could navigate the waters on our own. The gyroscope and ballast were tossed overboard and now we drift aimlessly in dangerous waters, swiftly approaching ominous reefs which lie in wait, our planet-ship so very close, so tragically unsuspecting.

Our present circumstance is indeed "a sleep and a forgetting." No longer does "life's star" illumine our way. The "celestial light" has slipped behind the clouds, no longer bright to guide us and keep us clear on course. Still we trail "clouds of glory," hidden from our consciousness. Yet even in our sleep and in our forgetting, God calls us still—calls us sweetly, gently home.

In turning our value systems upside down, we have secularized life to the extreme, opting for a life of vain hopes and illusion that constantly disappoint and frustrate. In the evolving Mystical Age, humanity will recover the sacred view, which will be not only our salvation but also our freedom and joy. We will be renewed and gifted anew with a sacred view of life when we have confronted our Mystery and penetrated our Deep and discovered the Divine Mother once again, Hagia Sophia, the Sacred Feminine.

We have conjured up ghostly apparitions in place of the lost vision of the sacred. This illusion lures us to pursue every new fad—spiritual or otherwise—every novelty, every enticement that beckons our way. The more we pursue the illusion, the more we are ultimately frustrated and disillusioned. Yet, mindlessly, we renew our empty pursuit with ever greater vigor and, with fierce determination, attempt to make our ghostly goal real and attainable. Thus we are drawn into a swishing whirlpool of vain hopes and shattered dreams.

If there is one word for what is driving us, it is *diversion*—our seemingly desperate need to escape reality, wasting our energies on everything except what is real, true, and vital. The media plays us like a master violinist, knowing every note to play and every string to pluck that will entice us and further mislead us. Buried beneath this need to be constantly diverted are fear and anxiety—an *angst* churning within that is the result of our true inner self being starved to death, fed an incessant diet of everything bland and vacuous. There is also deep-seated guilt, a guilt thrust upon us by our true self, which is quietly, secretly admonishing us for our falsity and infidelity. It yearns to break free.

Our true self is subject to one low- or high-voltage shock treatment after the other, numbing it but incapable of killing it—for our true self depends not on the harvest of nutritionless fodder to sustain it but on the love that is its ground and source. In the emerging new consciousness, once our true self is rescued from the barbarous attacks of the exterior self, men and women will recover the sacred view of life. Then will our own sacredness begin to shine. Then will we be free to reach out to others in compassion, and help heal our broken and tortured world.

Thomas Merton writes:

The sacred attitude is one which does not recoil from our own interior emptiness, but rather penetrates into it with awe and reverence, and with the awareness of mystery.

By virtue of the hidden presence of the Holy Spirit in our inmost self, we need only to deliver ourselves from preoccupation with our external, selfish and illusory self in order to find God within us.

The sacred attitude penetrates into that darkness and that nothingness, realizing that the mercy of God has transformed our nothingness into his temple, and believing that in our darkness his light has hidden itself.[1]

Within our Mystery and our Deep is the inner door that opens out into that celestial light. The light is free and is offered all who seek— for all who seek will find. It is offered to all who knock, for to all who knock, the door will be opened. We must seek as though we have already found, and knock as though the door has already been opened to us. What we wish to become, we are already. It is a matter of doing some digging, of mining the solitude of our hearts if our true inner self is to make some unexpected manifestation of itself.

> The Spirit and the Bride say, "Come."
> Let everyone listening say, "Come."
> All who desire it may have the water of life,
> and have it free.
>
> —Rev. 22:17

19 ❧ Living Time-free

It is only with the advent of the present but passing mental consciousness structure that we finally encounter conceptual time, which is quantitative and therefore can be referred to as "clock time." Here, for the
first time, a sharp delineation is made between past, present and future.
                                                        —Enomiya-Lassalle[1]

Twentieth-century men and women are mortgaged to time, slaves to
"clock time," which mercilessly controls and carves up our existence
into disparate pieces, driving us relentlessly and often pointlessly. In
the arising Mystical Age we will learn to become "time-free," to live
in the present moment, in a state of *mindfulness*, the key that
unlocks the "time-prison" that encloses us. We will come to live in
and experience the "sacrament of the present moment" (Jean-Pierre
de Caussade) and be open to receive God's grace, which is accessed
only in the "now moments" of life.

There is an Arabic saying that goes: "One cannot mount the camel
that has not yet arrived, nor the camel that has already passed."
Grace, which is God 's personal action upon us, can only be accessed
and experienced in life's "now moments." Dwelling on yesterday and
star-gazing into tomorrow are the "demons" that keep us scattered,
pulling us in all directions. This, in turn, prevents us from being
authentic, for our deep true self is buried under an avalanche of surface debris unleashed by our mental meanderings. This not only creates a state of interior chaos but is a form of violence to our true
inner self.

If we want to be liberated from the affliction at which we have arrived
through a consciousness where only "clock time" has any validity, we
must free time from this rational violence.
                                                        —Enomiya-Lassalle[2]

When Lassalle writes that "we must free time," he means not elim-
inating time but *transcending* our quantitative, mechanistic under-

standing of time, thus freeing both time and ourselves from the prison of purely quantitative-rationalistic thinking. "What does freedom from time mean?" he asks. "It means that time is no longer a threat, which is something that will be possible once we live more fully in the present moment."[3] Living in the past and constantly scanning the "what if" horizons of the past and future not only keep us from being authentic but create a drain on our vital energy. This life-force energy is being wasted and dissipated on phantasms, since past events and future possibilities are simply projections of our imagination, and are therefore unreal. *The only time an event is real is during the now-moment of its happening.* Part of this fruitless process is conjuring up Pollyanna thoughts such as: "If only things could be like...," "Wish I could be like so-and-so...," "If only this would not have happened...."

Thus we submerge ourselves in an imaginary, swirling tank of wishful thinking. All of this is not only wasteful of our energies but propels us into a no-man's-land, a land of make-believe, a wonderland of unreality. Nothing could be more injurious to spiritual growth and inner transformation. At the same time, we sweat and worry over "not having enough time," taking anxious note of every hour of our apparent lack of time. This creates a real *angst* and, instead of increasing our efficiency, works against it.

Time, of course, did not always exist. Time had a beginning, prior to which there was nothing. When the first words of the book of Genesis say, "In the beginning...," the author is referring to the Big Bang of perhaps some fifteen billion years ago. Before the Big Bang *nothing* existed; not time, not space.[4]

Einstein has shown that time and space have an integral relationship, are "interlocked," so to speak. Neither can exist without the other. We cannot say "before the beginning," since there *is* no "before," a word that is a constituent of time. The mind cannot conceive of no time and no space, since it has nothing (*no-thing*) to contemplate or reflect on. Thus, when St. Paul writes in the opening lines of Ephesians, "Before the world was made, God the Father chose us, chose us in Christ, to be holy and spotless and to live through love in his presence," he is saying, "In eternity (understood as the 'eternal present') the Godhead contained within himself, in the

Word, the Big Bang and all of creation." You and I eternally existed *in potencia* but not in "time." We "nested" in the "bosom of the Father," in the "eternal now" of eternity, known by God and loved by God. After billions of years following the genesis of time (the Big Bang), we came into space-time. We cannot ask, When did God decide to act and create the cosmos? since there is no "when." "When" belongs to time. God is beyond time. God is beyond being. God is emptiness, yet beyond and behind emptiness.

Attempting to comprehend such thoughts intellectually will only lead to migraines! We can ask Why? if we wish, but that question has baffled humankind since the dawn of the race. So why ask Why? Life, as has been said, is not a problem to be figured out but a mystery to be lived. As long as we continue trying to figure it all out, we will only lose ourselves in a labyrinth of absurdity and confusion. Whether we like it or not, realize it or not, we are participants in the cosmic dance. We are dervishes dancing to the music of the spheres, brothers and sisters of the stars carrying their constituent elements in our very bodies. We are one with the universe, God's playground, but don't know it. We are *star people*—people literally and truly one with the cosmos.

> In the playground of this world
> In joy, in suffering,
> I have beheld in sudden flashes
> The Infinite behind the veil of the finite;
> The meaning of my birth lay
> In that Beauty ineffable,
> In that Song inexpressible!
> When the drama ends,
> I shall leave behind
> In this earth's temple,
> My salutation.
> My worship.
> Whose value death cannot grasp.
>
> —Tagore, "The End"

An aspect of living "time-free" is developing an *inner eye of transparency*, which penetrates through words and concepts to the

essence of things, and which, as Enomiya-Lassalle points out, is not
the result of rational deduction:

> When we want to understand the essence of things, it is our habit to
> think about them: we take things apart to "analyze" and seek the
> ground of their existence.[5]

Such analytical/deductive thinking can reveal only a partial understanding of things; it can never penetrate to their essence. The development of "transparent seeing" can be learned through the faithful
practice of meditation. This usually entails a discipline of nonobjective meditation over a long period of time. (See chapter "Right
Meditation.") Our purely rational way of thinking (the dominant
characteristic of the departing present mental consciousness structure) must give way to a higher, superior way of thinking—mystical-
intuitive thinking. (See chapter "The New Thinking.")

Meanwhile, what to do about our scatteredness? For it slams shut
the door in our faces, locking us out of the fourth spiritual dimension. The answer lies in the practice of *mindfulness*, when, for at least
short periods of the day, we seize the reins of our galloping mind and
bridle its runaway tendencies. This means training ourselves to pay
attention to what we are doing at a particular time, during the activities of the day. There is a Latin saying, *Age quod agis*, which means,
"What you do, do that." (See chapter "The Forgotten Virtue.")

This means being totally present to the task at hand, and being
fully aware at each moment in which we are occupied by a certain
task or activity. It means *being alive!* It means not being lost in the
cyberspace of the imagination. It is what Zen meditation is all about.
It is what Buddhist "insight meditation" is all about. It is what
Christian contemplative prayer and centered living are all about.

The practice of mindfulness is a tough practice, as anyone who has
attempted this practice well knows. Our Western culture refuses to
honor mindfulness, except the mystics. Indeed, one cannot be a mystic without living in a more or less continual state of mindfulness, of
honoring the "sacrament of the present moment." We are products of
a culture that has created Westerners, "verbalizing animals" and "per-
petual ruminating machines."

Although we think of our disparate lives and activities as "reality," we have become a fragmented society without aim or direction, bending to every wind that blows our way, latching onto whatever is currently faddish, and caught in a vortex that spirals constantly downward into the black hole of oblivion.

Meister Eckhart puts all of this in the context of doing God's will perfectly and fulfilling the petitionary phrase in the Our Father that God's will be done:

> In the (present) moment, wait for God and follow him alone in the light he wishes to show you, through doing and letting go, and be so free and new in each moment, as if there was nothing else you wanted to do or could do other than what is given you and expected of you in this moment—for this is the fruit of God's birth.

20 § The New Thinking

Our age, more than any other, is pushing toward a new way of think-ing. It is a violent change that will bring into question much of what, up to now, has seemed to be a matter of course. At work in this drive is a longing for truth and reality.

—Enomiya-Lassalle[1]

Mythologist Joseph Campbell urged us to "follow your bliss!" To fol-low one's bliss is to often follow one's intuitions, which, by another name, are called "inspirations." Intuitions are information that come to us in energetic form. We can think of them as "noetic guidance" (*knowing* guidance).

In the new consciousness, the new thinking will be mystical-intuitive thinking, which will integrate present and past ways of think-ing. Old ways of thinking will be *integrated* in the new thinking and placed in the service of intuitive-mystical thinking. What we do, we will do more quickly, and more efficiently—when we are "heart-grounded."

Karl Jaspers calls this *transcendental thinking*, thinking that does not cleave to objects:

It goes beyond the intellect to the source of thinking itself. It rises ... from an all-encompassing presence, nor is it driven by the thing it tran-scends. It is drawn where it is going.[2]

The "violent change" of which Enomiya-Lassalle speaks will be our struggle to tear ourselves away from conventional modes of thinking that block out a vast portion of reality. Human reason alone is no longer adequate and is, in fact, obsolete and obstructs the bright future of humankind.

When the new consciousness is integrated, our innate "conduits of intuition" will be opened up, no longer suppressed by the rational mind that whispers: "intuition cannot be trusted—you must only do

75

what is rationally logical." All of us are born with intuitive powers and potencies. Intuitions are coming through all the time, but we have been taught to suppress them and have been told we must function "logically." Intuitions, modern, rationalistic culture tells us, are not to be trusted. Only the "reasoning mind," only logic and practicality must be followed.

We must separate ourselves from such "tribal thinking" and resist being swayed by society's three-dimensional conventional ways. This requires courage, which must come from the deep conviction that intuition indeed *can* be trusted and is truly a reliable guiding star. Intuition has nothing to do with spirituality. It has been pointed out that some of the best con men are exceptionally intuitive, experts at "reading" their victims before moving in for "the close" (or, more accurately, "the kill"). To follow one's intuitions implies certain risks, but risks we must take if we are to be freed from the constraints of conventional ways of thinking and conducting our lives. Intuitions do not come clothed in the protective armor of shining certitude. Giving up our rational control from time to time is the price we must pay in order to follow this guiding star, this illuminating light of "higher knowing."

The same is true in the spiritual life. There can be no breakthrough into the mystical dimensions of the spiritual journey without surrendering our need to be always in control. Surrendering control is exactly what is necessary to enter a new, higher stage of the spiritual life, to enter the new consciousness. "Surrender" doesn't mean to be irrational—it means to be *more* rational, only in a higher, deeper, more fruitful sense.

Thus the motto of Meister Eckhart: *Wiltu den kernen haben, so muost du die schalen breken,* "If you want the kernel, you must break the shell." If we want the kernel of life, the hard surface shell of our ordinary consciousness must be broken open, which it can never be as long as we insist on always being "in control."

Intuitive thinking does not involve a process of "by degrees." It is *instantaneous* in its manifestations. It spontaneously "happens"—when one is walking along the street, driving a car, sitting in meditation, having a quiet supper, waking up in the middle of the night—one is suddenly struck by an intuition. Intuition comes when it wishes, regardless of our employment at the time. We must therefore train ourselves to be always ready for it and to welcome it when one of those unexpected "inspirational moments" occurs.

Intuitions may sometimes arrive simultaneously in "bunches"—two or three inspirations that deposit themselves on our interior doorstep all at once, waiting to be welcomed and invited in. This can happen, for example, when one is writing a book or composing music. Several ideas will hit simultaneously, and one must scribble them down quickly or perhaps lose one or more of them. I am convinced that Mozart was literally inundated with "clusters" of musical ideas all at once. All true geniuses experience "cluster moments" of inspiration. Indeed, there never was a genius who did not move by the noetic energies of inspirations. Some inspirations can be most powerful and persuasive. When Tchaikovsky was asked why he composed music, he replied: "I write what I am compelled to write."

Intuitions are deep promptings of the heart to "come, follow me." "The heart has reasons," Pascal wrote, "that the mind does not understand." We must not, however, mistake temporary "feelings" or fleeting sensations for intuition. Intuitions come from a place much deeper than that. They are not whims or passing fancies; they carry a certain reality, a certain integrity, a certain urgency, a certain truthfulness. They are "sacraments" given to illuminate and guide us. Our intuitions need to be honored and welcomed, not ignored and dismissed.

The new thinking can say no more to those who want nothing but plans and instructions, but it will aid people perplexed by the ultimate aimlessness of all planned aims. For they have experienced the intellect's inability to guide the life of existence and resolution. Unless they drown their puzzled thoughts in the din of distracted and trivial activities, they will be saved by the thought processes of the new way—which are true only when the thinker changes.

—Karl Jaspers[3]

21 ❧ A New Church

The Christian Church has, for many centuries, given up its vital responsibility to create living mystics of great attainment. It has concentrated
on the external without doing the essential work of transformation.
                                                              —Andrew Harvey[1]

It is easy to criticize the Church, but never pleasant. Those of us who
are her sons and daughters must level such criticism with care, compassion, and charity, being careful not to "offend the Spirit" who is
its source and ground. The Church must be open to the criticism not
only of its own faithful but also to that of those outside the Church
who, nonetheless, have a concern for the Church if for no other reason than that the Church has such widespread influence on the world
at large.

As we level our criticisms at the Church, it is important we do not
become "Christian Pharisees," building up our own private fortress
of self-righteousness and believing ours to be the only true vision of
the Church. This can evolve into an odious morality; a stoic cynicism
and abject contempt for the "way things are presently"—rather than
taking up the spiritual courage of becoming people of deep prayer,
first radically transforming ourselves.

For many Catholics the present period of change in the Church
since Vatican II (one of the identifying marks of the new consciousness) is upsetting and confusing. Many feel that a "cozy home" has
fallen down around their ears. To begin with, the Church was never
meant to be a "cozy home," but a *koinōnia*, a community of disciples
faithful to their founder's teachings and example—this is to say, an
ecclesia whose members are lovers of God and neighbor, ready to
deny themselves (luxury, pleasures, power) and pick up their cross
daily (duties, sacrifices, and responsibilities, great and small, with all
their aggravating annoyances) and to do so without bitterness and
resentment. To be able to do this is to understand that, by grace, we

have advanced well along the spiritual journey. Those that do so with a certain joy are what are called "saints."

As the new consciousness unfolds, the Church will (must) undergo a radical mutation of structure and ways of teaching. It can no longer remain frozen in an obsolete medieval structure, nor proclaim the teachings of the gospel in language reminiscent of an exhausted Augustinian Neoplatonism. Thomas Merton was perhaps a century ahead of his time, bringing the message of the gospel to people in a new, fourth-dimensional way. He vibrated with thousands who were hungry for something more satisfying and more nurturing than the juiceless, unadorned rehashing of theological statements and doctrinal formulae.

It must be remembered that the bulk of the formulations of Church dogma came into existence at the peak of rational Greek (Aristotelian) thought. Almost all of the Church's foundational doctrines were "put to bed" during the first four of the seven Ecumenical Councils (fourth–fifth centuries), when dualistic Greek thought still reigned supreme. Jung advanced the consideration that the development of Christian theology since the introduction of Augustine and Aquinas has consistently led to the loss of the inner sense of God.

The theology of the Church is Greek, its organization Roman, and its cultural expression European. Therefore, it is not yet catholic (universal) in its form and structure and, as a result, cannot yet speak convincingly and coherently to Everyman.

Episcopal priest and Jungian psychologist John A. Sanford writes:

> The sense of the numinous is all but lost upon modern Christians; and in psychology the mysteries of the soul are dismissed in favor of rationalistic explanations for human behavior and problems.[2]

Such aperspectival thinking has even infected the way most Christians pray:

> Western Christianity has based its prayer forms largely on an exhausted scholastic philosophy and theology concerning human beings, God and the material world. A spiritual vision is needed to break through this Augustinian Platonism.
>
> —George A. Maloney[3]

The "new Church" must speak "mystically" from "the heart," not only rationalistically. "Head-talk" has for too long kept Christians from a direct, intuitive mystical experience of the Divine. Theology can only tell us something *about* God—experience brings a knowledge *of* God that causes all the "God-talk," all theology, to crumble and turn to dust.

> The conceptual representation of religious truths is no longer sufficient even for upright Christians. Many of these people no longer look to theology for their healing; they turn to different ways of experiencing God for themselves.
>
> —Enomiya Lassalle[4]

Thomas Aquinas dramatically discovered the hollowness of theology *per se* when, toward the end of his life, he had a profound mystical experience when praying before the crucifix. He would afterwards proclaim that everything he had written was "straw." The mystical experience of Aquinas was so powerful that it caused him not to speak or write during the last years of his life. He had seen the *shekinah*, the glory of God, which reduced to straw everything he had written.

The direct, intuitive, mystical experience of God cannot be mediated via statements and declarations, books and sermons—because words, thoughts, concepts and formulations are on the rational third-dimensional plane where God cannot be accessed and held close by an experience in the ground of one's being. This does not suggest that the rational mind will become obsolete, only that it will serve and be subservient to the new consciousness: "With this new consciousness, man will become a mystic, but one who awakens the mystical presence along with the use of reason."[5]

As Jung pointed out, the unavoidable truth remains that there is in humankind a deep need for the transcendent, a hunger that cannot be satisfied with theological statements and doctrinal imperatives. "Faith," wrote Jung, "is no adequate substitute for inner experience." Faith must deepen to where it is heart-grounded and not just an asset of the intellect.

> The individual will never find the real justification for his existence and his own spiritual and moral autonomy anywhere except in an extra-mundane principle. The individual . . . needs the evidence of inner tran-

scendent experience which alone can protect him from the otherwise inevitable submersion in the mass.[6]

This is humanity's greatest, deepest thirst, which cannot be assuaged except by the infused experience of the Divine. The living water that will parch our thirst lies deep in the wellspring of our inner being, Our *angst* can be assuaged only by an experience of the transcendent, by a heart awake and alive with love. This is not what the Church has been primarily concerned with over recent centuries. However, as Jung foresees, there is indeed hope for the Church:

I am convinced that it is not Christianity, but our conception of it that has become antiquated. The Christian symbol is a living thing that carries in itself the seeds of further development.[7]

In reflecting on the parable of the woman in the Gospel who lost one of her coins, William Johnston likens the woman to the Church and the lost coin to her lost contemplative heritage. The parable, as we know, says that the woman turned her house upside down in order to find the lost coin. So too, the Church must turn itself upside down and rummage through the basement of her house, searching the roots of her beginnings to rediscover the lost coin of her contemplative tradition.

Many who still attend church (a rapidly dwindling group) do not have inner contact with the Church—do not drink from the underground river that flows through the Church and keeps it from drying up. This underground river is the Spirit, who flows silently, deeply within the Church, which many talk about but few truly experience. The fire which Christ came to cast upon the earth (Lk. 12:49) still waits to be widely set ablaze in Christian hearts. If this were not so, the Church would have long ago transformed the world.

Although Vatican II attempted valiantly to revitalize and reorient its method of mission, it has yet largely failed to do so. Why is this so? Because, at the level of the magisterium—and sifting on down to the diocesan and parish levels, where the teaching Church meets the people—we are still subject to three-dimensional thinking and antiquated ways of teaching. This must change. But it cannot change until those who have been appointed "shepherds of the flock" are themselves inwardly transformed and drawn into the new consciousness. Today it is primarily lay contemplatives who are leading the Church into mystical consciousness. If the Church cannot create mystics, then the whole operation should be shut down, because a Church that cannot create mystics cannot represent itself as the Church of its founder.

Karl Rahner's inquiry remains crucially valid in our day:

> Where are there still the spiritual fathers, the Christian gurus, who possess the charisma of initiating into meditation and even into mysticism in which man's ultimate reality–his union with God–is accepted in a holy courage? Where are the people who have the courage to be disciples of such spiritual fathers?[8]

Just as the mutation of humankind from the mental to the mystical consciousness structure must necessarily be accompanied by suffering and dislocation, so too the Church must endure anguish and pain as it mutates to a new form, a new paradigm. This must be so for all of the world's great religions, which, along with the expanding evolution of humankind, must mutate alongside and together with humankind. Otherwise, religion as we know it will become a museum piece.

Christianity will probably be most impacted, since its structure is most rigid and authoritarian. Christianity must search deeply for its roots, probing the lived experience of those who walked with Jesus Christ on earth, of the fledgling communities that sprang up around the apostles, and of the early charismatic teachers and mystics. This must somehow culminate in a direct communication of the Holy Spirit, the "foundress" and nurturing mother of Christianity.

> If there is any assurance (of the success of the search) it can only lie in the individual religious experience encountered in deep prayer and contemplation. It is only here that the answer has a chance of coming directly from Christ.
>
> —Enomiya-Lassalle[9]

The turn of the West to the East in its serious study of Eastern spiritual paths has been one of the most important events of our time. As a result, Christians are becoming better Christians, not less. East and the West are "holding hands." This too is a sign and mark of the emerging new consciousness. The bonds of brotherhood, transcending racial, religious, and cultural boundaries, will be one of the pillars of the new consciousness structure. For the Church, it means walking into the future without a blueprint.

We must recognize soberly that no planning of the Church's future can relieve us of the necessity of going forward into a future that cannot be planned—of risk, of danger, and of hope in the incalculable grace of God. Even now we are going towards a future of the Church that is still hidden from us.

—Karl Rahner[10]

22 & The Fall of Fundamentalism

Most people think of fundamentalism as a primitive social trait, a dying holdout from an earlier age. But fundamentalism is not an old-world tradition. Only in recent times has there been a (Christian) movement whose theological platform has only one plank: the elevation of Scripture to a position of supernatural authority over all matters of faith, knowledge and everyday life. It is in this unquestioning of the Scriptures that fundamentalists part company with other Christians.

—Flo Conway[1]

In the path of the arising new consciousness is the opaque one-dimensional specter of fundamentalism, the ultimate product in religion of linear, left-brain thinking. These self-righteous forces deny and denounce whatever is not stamped in their own superficially etched image and likeness. Fundamentalism, it may be added, is generously coated with the slick film of intimidation and coercion.

Such forces exist in all of the world's religions, with the possible exception of Buddhism (which, however, is not, strictly speaking, a "religion"). The face of fundamentalism is a death mask in the process of taking shape, for it will not be able to withstand the incoming tide of the Mystical Age. Fundamentalism is anything *but* mystical.

Fundamentalists appear not so much to assert God as to assert themselves. It is sometimes difficult to discern what fundamentalists stand for, except that they are *for* Jesus and *against* sin. Frozen within the narrow passageways of linear thinking, fundamentalism often manifests itself in ugly ways: prejudice, hatred, persecution, outbreaks of widespread violence, sometimes mass hysteria. Fundamentalists are experts at left-brain thinking, a myopic one-dimensional view of things that gives rise to rigidity, which in turn creates absolutism, which in turn establishes one in self-righteousness, which is the sin of spiritual pride, the greatest sin. From then on it becomes a matter of projecting their "shadow" upon the rest of the human community.

Fundamentalism is a left-brain foray into the tremendously diverse country of religion that shuts out wisdom and bars the healing salve of openness and understanding. Our twentieth century and times past have been horribly scarred by the uglier manifestations of worldwide fundamentalism.

Remnants of fundamentalism will remain, holding tightly to their static beliefs in a desperate attempt to survive the tidal wave of the new paradigm. They will quote biblical verses out of context with vociferous passion in an effort to reinforce their positions and insulate themselves from the reality washing over and around them. These remnants will become the "religious barbarians" of the evolving new epoch—the religious Vandals and Visigoths of an age they cannot understand and refuse to deal with, except to rebel. The more the new consciousness develops and is integrated, the louder and more frequent will be the lamentations of fundamentalism.

In the Catholic Church, fundamentalism is very much alive, but struggling against the tide of the higher consciousness unleashed by Vatican II. A recent newspaper article recounted the experience of an author who tried to meet with the heads of several conservative Catholic organizations. Speaking on the phone to a member of one such group who refused to meet with her, she asked: "What will it take for us to meet?" The response came back: "I will meet with you only if we agree that absolute truth exists and that our work is to dedicate ourselves to that truth."[2]

We here direct our attention to Christian fundamentalism in general and look to its underlying error. Its "opaqueness" lies in the inability to see behind the words of scripture which it is so fond of quoting at the drop of a hat, failing to divine scripture's hidden, deeper, richer meanings beyond the obvious and literal. The Gospel is made up largely of stories and symbols (right-brain material) that the fundamentalist seems incapable of reading in this way. To quote the great Origen:

> The Scriptures ... have a meaning not only as is apparent at first sight, but also another which escapes notice of most. For these words which are written are the forms of certain mysteries, the image of divine things.[3]

Addressing the purely literal interpretation of Scripture, Thomas Merton writes:

> What is hidden beneath the literal meaning is not merely another and more hidden meaning; it is also a new and totally different reality ... it is the divine life itself. ... The spiritual understanding of Scripture leads to a mystical awareness of the Spirit of God himself living and working in our souls, carrying out by his mysterious power in our own lives the same salvific actions prefigured and realized in the Old and New Testaments.[4]

The foremost biblical scholars of our day agree that the first eleven chapters of Genesis are myth. Don't ever tell a fundamentalist that the story of Noah and the ark is only that, a story, a myth (which nonetheless veils a hidden truth). The search for Noah's ark can go on from now until doomsday and it will never be found—because it never existed! Ignoring all the great advances in scriptural exegesis in the latter part of this century (form criticism, historical-critical exegesis, and so on), fundamentalists refuse to acknowledge the validity of these methods—tools of biblical exegesis that have advanced our understanding of scripture more in the last six decades than in all nineteen preceding centuries. Commenting on the Gospel of John, Raymond E. Brown, a preeminent biblical scholar of our time, writes what is also applicable to the Synoptic Gospel accounts: "The Gospel must be read on several levels, so that it tells us both the story of Jesus and the community that believed in him."[5]

The fundamentalist continually waves one or two out-of-context Gospel passages in front of us, stretching them beyond all valid interpretation and meaning. Thus the quotation "No one comes to the Father except through me" (John 14:6) is often used to declare that no one except the Christian can attain to God—or for that matter be "saved." This we know is nonsense. In opposition to the fundamentalist insistence on the historical accuracy of scripture, Brown warns that "a Gospel may be used only with great circumspection as a historical source." Those who wrote the Gospels were writing not as historians but as conveyers of *selected* events and sayings of Jesus they felt were important and relevant *to the communities they were writing to.*

Primarily, the Gospels tell us how an evangelist conceived of and presented Jesus to a first century Christian community, a presentation that indirectly gives us an insight into that community's life at the time when the Gospel was written.[6]

When the Divine Mother gathers up her harvest during the decades ahead, the chaff of fundamentalism will be separated from the good wheat of the new consciousness and left by the wayside—or else it will be taken up and changed into it. The fervor of fundamentalist single-mindedness and the "war on sin" (a favorite topic) is characterized by evangelist Billy Sunday, who was "against sin":

I'm against sin. I'll kick it as long as I've got a foot, and I'll fight it as long as I've got a fist. I'll butt it along as long as I've got a head. I'll bite it as long as I've got a tooth. And when I'm old and listless and footless and toothless, I'll gum it till I go home to Glory and it goes home to perdition.[7]

23 🎋 All Things Inter-Are

No speck so tiny is,
no spark can be so dim.
The wise man does not see
God's splendor deep within.
                    —Angelus Silesius[1]

In Christianity, the myth of "the fall" is the fall of humankind out of unitive consciousness into divided consciousness.[2] Eating from the tree of knowledge (the tree of discrimination) is the symbol for separation and alienation, a tree that gave forth its bitter fruit of divided consciousness, of alienation, and hurled humankind into the dark dungeon of constant self-reflection and self-absorption.

Paradise lost is the shipwreck of humanity on the shoals of a divided consciousness, on the coral reefs of a "split psyche." No longer would men and women see each other, or the world around them, as one. "Me," "mine," and "not yours" would become the language of separateness, the speech of divided consciousness, the voice of endless dualities.

Is it you or I
this reality in the eye?
Beware, beware
of the word "two."
                    —al Hallaj

Thich Nhat Hanh gives us an illuminating example of unitive consciousness:

Without a cloud, there will be no rain; without rain, the trees cannot grow; and without trees, we cannot make paper. The cloud is essential for the paper to exist. So we can say that the cloud and the paper inter-are.[3]

Martin Buber writes that the sin of Adam was that he wanted to "do good"—on the face of it, a perplexing statement. Buber is saying that Adam (early humanity) *needed to know* when he was "doing good." Prior to this, Adam simply went about his life doing all the things he was doing without reflecting on whether or not his actions were good or bad. He lived in the "Eden of unitive consciousness," one with God, with the animals, with all that was his world.

In Christianity, Eden is the symbol for one's true home, a state of being of unitive consciousness. The "fall" is the Big Bang of human experience, which ruptured our unitive consciousness, breaking it into ten thousand pieces and fragments, hurling us into the confused and illusionary world of dualities. More than that, it ultimately led to the "hyper-individuated" person, the creation of the false god of the small self. Humankind, at least in the West, has usurped God's throne, and, in God's place, has enthroned the Baal of individualism, the god of the empirical ego.

Franciscan Richard Rohr recounts a story told him by a young couple. The couple had just brought home a new baby, the infant brother of another child, Tommy, who was about four years old. After they placed the new baby in a bassinet, Tommy asked if he could speak to his new baby brother, to which the parents agreed. "But I want to speak to him alone," said the youngster. The couple hesitated a moment but agreed. They let him into the room where the new baby lay, but protectively eavesdropped through a crack in the bedroom door. This is what they heard Tommy say: "Quick, Christopher, tell me who I am ... tell me who God is, because I'm starting to forget!" Tommy was losing his unitive consciousness, losing his memory of his prebirth experience of coming from a "place divine." Tommy was losing his "original face" of before he was born.

The poem "Prelude" by William Wordsworth is apt indeed, alluding to our forgetting, the farther away we move from childhood innocence. Heaven indeed lies about us in our infancy, but as we grow older and "sophisticated" our guiding star fades into the common light of day. However, our pristine unitive consciousness has not been forever lost; it lies dormant in the deepest recesses of our being, within the true self, that "depth unvisited" by a society seemingly content to surf the whitecaps of life. We thus live outside the gates of Eden, our return guarded against by a cherub with "the flame of a flashing sword" (Gen. 3:24), the sharp differentiating saber of our divided consciousness.

The flaming sword can be extinguished and our return to Eden made possible when our "original blessing" is restored, when we are sufficiently open to again receive the celestial light that lay about us in our infancy. This return to Eden, to unitive consciousness, is known by different names—enlightenment, contemplation, the great compassion, the kingdom of God. Such are the gifts of the evolving mutation of consciousness, the gifts of new "gold, frankincense, and myrrh" from Wisdom, the Mother, bearer of the Mystical Age.

In Jewish mysticism, the *shekinah*, the shining presence of God, is throughout all creation and in every creature, like sparks that emanate from the Spirit-flame that is Yahweh. It is identified as the feminine principle of God: "The feminine principle is identified with the Divine Presence, the Shekinah, the essence of God that pervades all creation. It is the essence that is the true beauty of all things."[4]

The Divine Mother will not reveal her secrets or her gifts as long as we insist on living an exclusively left-brain existence, as long as we refuse to surrender control of every aspect of our lives. For this, great detachment is needed—detachment that will make it possible for us to resist the inviting siren wails of the world.

> Reasoning and discrimination vanish after the attainment of God and communion with him. How long does a man reason and discriminate? As long as he is conscious of the manifold, of "I" and "You." When he is truly aware of unity, he becomes silent.
>
> —Sri Ramakrishna[5]

24 ❧ Wedding Bells

Jesus said to them: "When you make the two one, and when you make the inside like the outside...you make the male and the female one and the same. Then you will enter the Kingdom."

—Gospel of Thomas[1]

Before the dawn of the new epoch can become the light of high noon, two sacred marriages must take place: the marriage of patriarchy and matriarchy, and the holy nuptials of the conscious and the unconscious. These marriages will take place virtually simultaneously, since these elements are already married in the divine consciousness. The ceremonies will take place in the chapel of our hearts—a double wedding—whose progeny will be the enlightened children of a new age.

While we cannot retreat thousands of years back to the matriarchal age, we can access certain of its qualities and attributes, for they are stored in the collective unconscious, the history book of humanity going back to the earliest days of our ancestors. The masculine powers of will, need for clarity and control, aggressiveness, and the demand for order and precision must be gradually integrated (balanced-married) with the feminine, nurturing powers of compassion, mercy, intuition, gentleness, openness, and love of nature.

It will, however, be a long engagement period, for the sacred marriages of which we speak will not be "love at first sight" and then off to Las Vegas for a quickie wedding! The entrenched patriarchal mindset of our present age will take time to break through, to be cracked open to allow innate feminine powers to arise from the collective and personal unconscious.

The cracks in patriarchy's seemingly impenetrable, thick walls have become obvious and visible to all with eyes to see. They will be the "disembarkation ports" whereby the feminine vanguard will breach the ramparts of the decaying fortress of patriarchy. Only the most dense and obstinate refuse to see that patriarchy has failed us. Unless it becomes balanced by the infusion of the feminine, life as we know it will disappear from our planet.

> The chaos and tragedy we are surrounded by makes it clear . . . that scientific rationalism and the cult of technological progress taken to fanatic lengths are suicidal, and that humankind dissociated from the wisdom of nature is doomed.
>
> —Andrew Harvey[2]

As the sacred marriage takes place, it must permeate every aspect of life, in all its variety and forms, not just in the spiritual arena or in isolated periods of prayer and meditation. It must diffuse itself and shed its light upon all the normal, everyday activities and pursuits of ordinary people engaged in ordinary things.

The second sacred marriage that must occur is the union of the conscious and the unconscious. Consciousness is pure awareness, not simply the awareness of things but, in a way, consciousness of itself. Consciousness is that by which we experience ourselves, through our five senses, our acts of reflecting, discriminating, deciding, and judging. Experiencing, understanding, and judging are the three basic stages of the knowing (consciousness) process. Whatever is fed into our consciousness influences the way we think and act. If our consciousness has been fed almost exclusively "male stuff," then our thinking and actions will be cast in the maleness mold, the patriarchal model.

Our unconscious is a vast "psychic sea" of all those myriad materials and components that we cannot voluntarily call up on the screen of our conscious mind. Deep within this psychic sea is the boiling pot of what Jung calls the "collective unconscious," and the equally volatile "shadow." Our unity and wholeness (individuation) depend on both layers, indeed all layers, of our psyche becoming integrated.

> We see that the unconscious is a seething mass of primitive images, passion, hate and resentment. In dreams and in insanity the veil is partly drawn aside . . . which can also be pulled aside by such techniques as hypnosis, drugs, psychotherapy etc. Deep prayer in the presence of an immanent God can also lead us into this inner world and bring about inner healing and the integration of the unconscious with the conscious.
>
> —George A. Maloney[3]

To become individuated—that is, to have an integrated personality— a harmonization of the different layers of our psyche must occur, what we are calling the "sacred marriage of the conscious and the unconscious." Part of the marriage ceremony is the unloading of the unconscious, of the repressed junk of a lifetime, and our acceptance of this repressed material as part of who we are. George A. Maloney points out that true religion allows us to "move into the hidden areas of the unconscious to make contact with one's genetic coding that is grounded in the numinous and sacred presence of God."[4]

Symbols (from the Greek *symbollein*, "to bring together") are an important part of the sacred marriage, for they bring together the conscious and the unconscious, informing us with vital new knowledge. Thus Carl Jung: "As the mind explores the symbol, it is led to ideas that lie beyond the grasp of reason."[5] To discover the deep reality of oneself is to discover the reality of God obscurely but numinously, the Divine Mother who is the ground and source of all being, what Merton has called "the hidden ground of Love."

> Don't dream this thread is double-ply:
> root and branch are but One.
> Look close: all is He—
> but He is manifest through me.
> All ME no doubt—
> but through him.
>
> But make no mistake:
> He who is lost in God
> is not God Himself.
>
> —Fahkruddin ʿIraqi

25 ❧ Radical Humility

> [Jesus] got up from the table, removed his outer garment and, taking a towel, wrapped it around his waist. He then poured water into a basin and began washing the feet of the disciples, wiping them with the towel he was wearing. He came to Simon Peter, who said to him: "Lord, are you going to wash my feet?" Jesus answered, "At the moment you do not know what I am doing, but later you will understand."
>
> "Never!" said Peter. "You shall never wash my feet!" Jesus replied: "If I do not wash your feet, you can have nothing in common with me."
>
> —John 13:4–8

Why have we forgotten to wash each other's feet? Why have we forgotten that if we do not serve others we can have nothing in common with Him?

Humility is not an attribute characteristic of our present age. Quite the contrary. Modern society holds humility in contempt, equating it with weakness, lack of self-confidence, even wimpishness. Humility, it proclaims, prevents expressing and asserting oneself, denying us the opportunity of self-fulfillment. Humility is not just one of other virtues. It is the "mother-virtue." The root meaning of *virtue* does not mean to be virtuous; it means *strength*, to be strong. Unless we build our house on the bedrock of humility, we might as well toss our spiritual house plans to the winds before we start. Humility (*humus* = earth) is the sacred ground in which the other virtues are rooted, the good soil that prepares us for grace and for growth. Without humility, the other virtues—the beams, connecting joists and bearing walls of our house—will have nothing upon which to be grounded.

In humility there is strength, because humility *is* strength—a strength that refuses to succumb to or be manipulated by the ego. To be blown about by the ego is to be driven by illusion. Illusion is nothingness. To be turned and twisted by nothingness is the most preposterous of weaknesses and the greatest of tragedies. In reality, it should be the ultimate humiliation and embarrassment—if only it could be recognized as such. The ego will pull every trick in the book to keep humility from sprouting and becoming the most beautiful of the spiritual adornments. Most importantly, the theological virtues of faith, hope, and love cannot be born in us without humility. They are called "theological" because they are infused directly by God, and God will not cast the pearls of these virtues before the snorting swine of pride, which will only turn on them in contempt and devour them in its arrogant disdain.

As the new evolutionary age dawns more brightly, radical humility will become one of its marks, for it must. Without radical humility, the Mystical Age will be extremely slow in developing. Instead of coming on us like rapidly successive ocean waves, it will creep tortoise-like upon humanity. Like stranded moored boats, humanity awaits the rising tide of a higher consciousness, hoping for a favorable wind, the *ruah* of God, to carry us back to Eden. Profound humility is necessary to be gifted with the experience of God. Unless we become as little children, we will be barred from the Kingdom within.

The road back to Eden, to switch metaphors, is constructed of the paving blocks of humility, giving it granite-like strength, depth, and directness of course. It follows a secret map sketched out by Holy Wisdom, and knows where the Holy Grail is to be found. Let us always seek and embrace this mother of all virtues, this humility, which alone can re-create us as little children and make us worthy to reenter Eden.

Humility can be birthed in us in different ways and under varying circumstances. It can take root in us as a result of a great crisis that we find ourselves helpless to resolve, whereby we experience the shattering of the sense of self-sufficiency that heretofore had always "gotten us through" past difficulties and problems. It can be born out of a love for another person that is so strong and deep that "the other" becomes far more important and cherished than our own life and concerns, forcing the ego to contract—for the ego cannot survive the reality of a great love.

Humility can reveal herself out of the awesome splendor of creation. The seas and the stars and the canopy of the cosmos may communicate to the see-er the Reality that proclaims: "I am—and *because* I am, you are!"

> His presence is a sun
> and heaven and earth
> I find are but a parasol.
> —Fahkruddin ʿIraqi

The Greek Fathers called this *theōria physikē*, the contemplation of God in the natural world. *Theōria physikē* means more than the outward perception. It is to see the "within-ness" of all created things, the inner radiance of the natural world. The deepest humility is born out of silence and solitude, in wordless, listening prayer in which we are brought, by grace, to experience that "in Him we live and breathe and have our being" (Gal. 2:20). This is true self-knowledge. Within the dark Cloud of Unknowing we are, paradoxically, given to know the unexplainable, the unutterable, the inexpressible, sometimes the unbearable.

We are given to experience the creative love of the Divine Feminine. We are given a taste, if only momentary, of what it means to come home to Eden.

> To the property of motherhood belong nature, love, wisdom and knowledge—and this is God.
> —Julian of Norwich

26 ❧ Radical Detachment

Anyone who would save his life will lose it.
                                        —Matt. 10:39

Jesus is speaking here about attachment, attachment that binds us to things, people, and pursuits and prevents us from being free, and loving freely. Attachment blinds, keeping us from seeing clearly, from seeing deeply. Just as the fourth spiritual dimension cannot be entered without deepened humility, so the new consciousness cannot be accessed without radical detachment. We must walk in both shoes of humility and detachment into the new epoch evolving around us and within us.

Detachment gives us a clarity of vision for what is real as well as a deep appreciation for the good things of life that are otherwise muddied and obscured by attachment, whereby we see only with the exterior eye. An interior vision is needed to penetrate the disguise of outward appearances, a vision that sees inwardly, sees the "sacred withinness" and therefore the newness and constant freshness of things, people, and events. This is not a form of pantheism in any sense but a simple gifted awareness that all life, animate and inanimate, is "charged with the grandeur of God" (John Courtney Murray), in whom all things subsist. Thus, everything is constantly being recreated and held in being in the cosmic matrix wherein all the different elements of the cosmos are, at the same time, relational and interdependent. They are different but not separate.

Detachment is not aloofness, is not a "cold shoulder" to the world. It is not callous indifference. Detachment frees us from the "stickiness" of worldly values and allurements. It frees us to love unconditionally, to become our true selves. It is a matter of distance and perspective, to be in the world but not of it. We renounce the world that Christ would not pray for in order to receive a higher joy by using the things of the world with a holy indifference, the way God means us to use and enjoy them. In a word, detachment is freedom.

The Dalai Lama says that even our love for our family members is a form of attachment—a "hard saying" that jars our sensibilities and common understanding. Yet, if we ponder deeply, we will become aware that our love of spouse, children, and parents is not pure, unconditional love but is conditioned by the fact that they are *ours*, that they *belong* to us. It is *my* brother, *my* sister, *my* spouse, *my* mother, *my* father. Undeniably, real love is present, but it is love biased by possessional attachment. The Dalai Lama's statement is not far removed from another "hard saying" found in the Gospel: "Anyone who prefers father or mother to me is not worthy of me. Anyone who prefers son or daughter to me is not worthy of me" (Matt. 10:37-38). Many of the "hard sayings" of the Gospel we too often rationalize down to more "realistic" and "reasonable" interpretations. The Gospel thus becomes relativized and minimalized. Halfhearted interpretations of the Gospel message make for halfhearted Christians. The narrow gate that leads to life is narrower than we prefer to think.

Possessional love diminishes the other person, for it robs that person of the complete freedom which makes people fully human. Not to free others from possessional love is to keep them imprisoned, unable to be fully free and to love fully. Radical detachment means not denying or fighting off deep attractions for others but bonding with them, not with the sticky glue of attachment but with a mutually free and shared heart-embrace that bonds yet does not bind.

All of this has something to do with "purity of heart," by which we are drawn closer to God because we understand that the treasured friendship of another is a gift, freely given and freely received. It is ours to be enjoyed and be enriched by, not a possession.

Jesus said he came to bring not peace but a sword (Matt. 10:35). The sword of which he speaks is the keen blade that cuts the knotted bond of attachment, freeing us to see reality and to love unconditionally—God, family, and friends. Thus we are able to "lose our life" in order to find our real life (Matt. 10:39), to shed our false self and allow our true self to become manifest. The person able to jettison unholy attachment will be gifted with a sacred view of life in all its wonder and richness. Once the barnacles of attachment are scraped away, our life's ship can loose its moorings and sail into the wide, open, limitless sea.

Transformative grace is offered us precisely for this task. The living waters of grace contain a powerful "solvent" able to gradually dissolve the "glue" of attachment. For the Christian, it is in the passively received Night of Sense that we first learn true detachment. In this night, the Spirit's gift of knowledge is infused, revealing the emptiness and hollowness of things in themselves. Fortified with this new experiential knowledge, we find we have little or no desire to pursue the passing superficial things of the world.[1]

It is something like a person who has always savored gourmet dining, only one day to have their taste buds surgically removed. From then on, eating is for nourishment only, not for pleasure. On the spiritual journey we ingest only those things along the way that will truly spiritually nourish us, finding a higher joy in them than what the senses alone can provide. Our senses, now sharpened and heightened, see more deeply, comprehend more profoundly, judge more astutely. We are now able to live more freely, fully, and completely.

All this must not be interpreted as life-denying or to suggest that one take up a harsh and inhuman asceticism of avoiding pleasure at all cost. It is a question of distance and discretion, of perspective and insight. We seek the real, the true, the meaningful. We shun the trivial, the false, the superficial. To achieve this is to have already achieved enlightenment. To achieve enlightenment is to awake from a dream-like state, where a thousand veils hide the radiance of truth.

O frozen Christian, awake!
—Angelus Silesius[2]

27 ❧ The Forgotten Virtue

Jesus said: "What I say to you, I say to all: Stay awake!

—Mark 13:37

Western Christianity has its litany of virtues, all neatly systematized.[1] What if we were to suggest that a most important "virtue" has been largely overlooked by the great teachers and theologians—the virtue of *mindfulness?* The practice of mindfulness is a form of meditation we must continually practice.

If mindfulness is to be considered a virtue, it must possess important characteristics of virtues as Christianity understands them. The virtues are those interior qualities which strengthen us (*virtus* = strong), by which we are spiritually renewed and strengthened, so that our "hidden self may grow strong" (Eph. 3:17), so that we may become "fully mature with the fullness of Christ himself" (Eph. 4:13). One can say that virtues are those spiritual energies which the Holy Spirit infuses along the spiritual journey to make us strong in Christ. For the Holy Spirit to work effectively in us, a certain inner peace and tranquillity must be developed which unify our scatteredness and bridle our tendencies to hurl ourselves into life's endless distractions. Mindfulness prepares us for enlightenment—in Christianity, to receive the gift of contemplation. One of the impediments to the gift of contemplation is being too "outward-minded"—that is, too tied to the world.

The practice of mindfulness leads to inner calm and unity of spirit, preparing the ground of our being to receive the seeds of life. One of the great viruses running rampant throughout American society is our compulsion to rush, to always be in a hurry to get things done. Americans have a way of "attacking" tasks and projects with a certain ferocity, almost as if someone or something is whipping us. This disease is thwarting the Spirit, refusing the Spirit entrance, denying us the time to attend to the needs of others in compassion, though they may be right in front of us.

For the Christian mystic, as his or her contemplative life deepens, one is drawn more and more into the present moment. The mystic begins to live in the "eternal now," in which mindfulness of the present moment becomes ever more habitual, ever more clarifying and translucent.

Mindfulness allows us to see deeply and so to see reality, to "touch" the "within-ness" of things and others. In the touching we are enriched with the gift of understanding. Understanding leads to harmony. Harmony leads to peace. Peace makes us children of God and citizens of the kingdom: "Blessed are the peacemakers for they shall be called the children of God" (Matt. 5:9).

"Stay awake!" Jesus said. The practice of mindfulness helps us to stay alert and awake. Thich Nhat Hanh says that, in so doing, we "touch" Jesus, we "touch" the Buddha. The Christ-I within us and our innate "Buddha nature" are themselves awakened and our living is transformed.

Mindfulness, like the Christian virtues, does not become a virtue without practice. As is the case with all virtues, the practice is difficult in the beginning, but gradually the practice becomes easier and eventually habitual. "Practice" is the operative word. If there is no practice, there can be no virtue. The virtue remains, but as a seed that never opens.

So we must practice the virtue of mindfulness. To repeat, it is not at all easy at first. In fact, our beginning practice is quite difficult. The practice requires courage and determination. Our minds are so used to running around all over creation that they have difficulty even comprehending the meaning of this strange word, mindfulness. Our mind is like a wild horse that has been lassoed and led into a corral. It must be trained. It must be broken of its wild habits. Otherwise the horse will trample us.

How do we start our practice? Let us recognize the fact that it is much easier to practice mindfulness in a monastery, or an ashram, or a Zendo, where silence is also considered a virtue and where we are together with others who are like-minded and dedicated. Practicing mindfulness by oneself requires greater courage, greater determination. But it can be gradually—ever so gradually—acquired over time. We should start with something we do every day and make a commitment that, during that activity, we will make the effort to be mindful. Gradually, we can extend the practice to other times and activities of the day.

Start perhaps with eating. When eating, try to be simply mindful that you are eating! We are tempted to engage in a distraction while eating, such as reading a newspaper or magazine or, worse, watching TV. Many of us don't really eat; we "glom down" our food while thinking of all the things we want to do later or tomorrow. Eating is sometimes almost an inconvenience, preventing us from getting on with other interests!

If we are eating with others, awareness of them and appreciating them become part of our mindfulness. They are "one" with this "now moment" of eating. Unless we are on retreat where there is silence during meals, we should exchange good conversation and friendship. This does not prevent us from being mindful that we are also eating. Listen to Thich Nhat Hanh:

> Mindful eating is an important practice. It nourishes awareness in us. We chew each morsel of food thoroughly... to help get us to be truly in touch with it. Eating this way is also good for digestion.
>
> Then we can look at the food deeply, in a way that allows it to become real. Contemplating our food before eating in mindfulness can be a real source of happiness. Every time I hold a bowl of rice, I know how fortunate I am. I know that thousands of children die every day because of the lack of food. I visualize them and feel deep compassion.[2]

Teachings on mindfulness are beginning to appear in the writings of current Christian authors, at least the contemplative ones. I do not believe this would be happening except for the influence of Buddhism, which has given Christians (who relish good theology!) a theology of mindfulness. It is one of the many wisdom teachings with which Buddhism has gifted Christianity. We must be open and learn from them so as to become better Christians.

> Breathing in, I calm my body.
> Breathing out, I smile.
> Dwelling in the present moment,
> I know this is a wonderful moment.
> —Thich Nhat Hanh[3]

28 ✿ The Emergence of Women

> The unfortunate resistance to today's feminism is not a resistance to
> undoing thousands of years of male obnoxiousness and female dupe-
> dom, but a resistance to the mergence of an *entirely new structure of
> consciousness.*
>
> —Ken Wilber[1]

As we consider the emergence of women in the present evolving age,
a look back in time is helpful in framing our observations.

During the Neolithic Age, about ten thousand years ago, men and
women collaborated as equals, joined by the duties and responsibilities that best suited each, male and female. Separation by *status* did
not exist. Differentiation was by *function.*

> At this early point, this differentiation (male-female) does not appear to
> be more important or more valued than the other. It appears to have
> been mostly a simple differentiation of function, not a massive differ-
> entiation of status.
>
> There is no evidence that it was intensely ideological or exploitive,
> but rather seems to have been based on such simple biological factors
> as physical strength and mobility (male advantage) and procreation and
> biological nursing (female advantage).
>
> —Ken Wilber[2]

Wilber notes that when the plow came along (requiring heavy
"muscular" work), there was a massive shift from a largely female
work force (using the light hand-held hoe) to one predominantly male,
spawning the transition from a horticultural to an agrarian society.
Wilber observes that "this aspect of the shift from matrifocal to patri-
focal [his terms] cannot reasonably be ascribed to oppression or male
domination."[3]

This transfer of functions eventually transmuted to a difference of
status as the male moved into the public sphere and the female was

relegated to the private-reproductive-nursing sphere. Anthropologists are generally agreed that during the Neolithic period society (tribes) was mostly matriarchal, and that a period of a dominant female culture extended over several thousands of years, times much less warlike and more integral than our own. Wilber notes: "Peggy Sunday has demonstrated that predominant female deity figures appear almost exclusively in (such) horticultural societies...whereas virtually all agrarian societies have male-only deities."[4] It is not difficult to see that, as male deities came to "rule" the world, it was an easy next step to the premise: If the gods are male, then women must be inferior to the male! Not an example of shining logic, but effective sleight-of-hand nonetheless!

Ken Wilber observes that when the male eventually undertook the role of father it heralded the emergence of the human family. He humorously and insightfully comments: "Thus began the one single nightmarish task of all subsequent civilizations...the taming of the testosterone!"

This history lesson behind us, we can now look at the emerging mutation of consciousness and its meaning and relevance for women in terms of justice, equality, and status. We might insert at this point the results of a series of studies at Yale University in 1996 which led to an auspicious discovery: studies reveal that when women speak, both hemispheres of the brain are at work, which is not the case with men. In their speech (therefore in their thinking) women are calling both left and right hemispheres into cooperative interplay. What this portends exactly is uncertain, except to suggest that women indeed see things differently from men, perhaps more wholly and "of a piece."

Obviously, we cannot go back ten thousand years to tribal times, to what is called "archaic consciousness." As the Mystical Age advances and becomes integrated, men and women are destined to once again become "integral" with each other, and the separation and oppression created by status will eventually become a chapter in history's dusty notebook.

We see this happening already in Western society, although certainly not yet on an expansive level playing field. It is, however, one of the identifiable marks of the emerging new consciousness. What is needed is more kindness and gentility on both sides, male and female, more understanding of how we have come to be the way we are, and more compassion, of which there seems to be too little at the present time. Vitriol, accusations, and bitterness will only "hold back the dawn" of a new day for womankind. "What is needed," reminds Jean Gebser, "is care, a great deal of patience and the laying aside of many preconceived notions."

The present times are often replete with bitterness and sometimes downright hatred between men and women. This poison of invective is evidence of the suffering and dislocation previously alluded to of humanity in transition from the Mental to the Mystical Age, from the three-dimensional to the fourth-dimensional structure. There is no other way for the "new baby" to be birthed except accompanied by the labor pains brought on by the mutation of the new consciousness.

The world's great religions, all having originated in the patriarchal age, have contributed greatly to the diminution of women. The Tibetan word for *woman* means "lesser birth." The Qurʾan is quite explicit in its declaration that women are inferior to man. The Sufi mystic Ibn al ʿArabi writes that "God loves women only because of their lower rank and being the repository of passivity." Both Augustine and Aquinas saw women as inferior to men. Hinduism, while lauding women in certain passages of the Vedas, has spawned one of the most odious and repressive of societies.

Thomas Merton viewed the oppression/suppression of women over the last four or five thousand years in terms of the "feminine mystique," the idealization of supposed feminine qualities which have been made much of over the centuries, causing women to be placed on a pedestal—and made to stay there! Merton remarks that women have been seen by men to be passive and mysterious. "To make a mystique out of something like this," he writes, "is nonsense."[5]

A new integration is now demanded on a social level, and viewing it in this evolutionary light allows us to bypass much of the standard and useless rhetoric that men have been oppressive pigs from day one, with the unavoidable implication that women have been herded sheep.

—Ken Wilber[6]

29 🎵 Swords into Plowshares

> They will hammer their swords into plowshares, their spears into sickles. Nation will not lift sword against nation; there will be no more training for war.
>
> —Isaiah 2:4

We will dismantle our missiles and atomic warheads; our nuclear submarines will return to port and be disassembled. We will empty our arsenals of "smart bombs" and the means to deliver them. Our military training bases will be turned into schools and low-cost housing for the poor. We will look back with horror upon what our fathers and forefathers wrought upon humanity and pray for forgiveness, believing that they really did not comprehend what they were doing. We will offer thanksgiving that the thousands of years of suffering and terror and of "man's inhumanity to man" have ended.

Of all the defining marks of the emerging new epoch, perhaps this is the most Pollyannish of them all. Those who have seen several global wars and countless regional conflicts visited upon humankind can be excused if they laugh to scorn the vision just offered, the vision of a world without war. The same factors that rule the stock market—fear and greed—also cause the eruptions of war, for such negative energies foster hatred and the demonizing of other peoples. Such hatred, such demonizing, are the projections of a people's collective shadow, actually revealing a hatred of themselves. The motivations of politicians are rooted in the same fear and greed. Clearly, a "new politics" must arise.

On a "good day," a Roman legion was capable of slaying perhaps a thousand or so men. It takes modern man but minutes to obliterate hundreds of thousands—and do so antiseptically, so that the screams and blood are out of sight and hearing. Such power becomes very "heady" for those who possess great stockpiles of potential destruction.

It is precisely this vision of a world without war that calls for patient optimism and courageous hope. The Light of the Mother will not somehow suddenly descend upon the masses. Her gifts will not be integrated into the collective consciousness in a day or in a year, but will require a long extended period of patience and courage until the possibility of global peace becomes the reality of the times. Finding and holding on to world peace must arise out of the transformation of consciousness of individuals first, and then their coming together as a community of higher consciousness.

> We must find the will and the way in the cooperation of all nations. This cooperation and great sacrifices—of glory, of prestige, of sovereignty, of material comfort, of privilege—are premises of survival. If they are forced upon us by events, the situation will be far more disastrous than if we reflect calmly, in time . . . and do freely what we recognize as unavoidable.
>
> —Karl Jaspers[1]

Inasmuch as the virulent strains of fear and greed are the root causes of war and violent conflict, it is clear where humanity must look for the antidotes. As the mutation to higher consciousness continues, a new sense of respect and understanding among nations will rise with it, bringing nations closer together in a genuine spirit of brotherhood and cooperation. It will become stunningly clear that the possibility of war, with its consequent agonies and sufferings, is no longer an option. Rogue countries that may still want to resort to violent action will be so completely cut off and isolated from the peace-loving family of nations that their very self-interest will compel them to behave in a manner consistent with the aspirations of the world community.

> Some will object—what fantastic expectations! Think of the reality of armaments! Are these huge efforts, consuming half the labor (and wealth) of nations, to have been "in vain"? Surely this whole vast output of energy rests on a serious purpose to resort to these weapons.
>
> And yet—if at first only under the growing stress of the fear that grips all men in view of its reality—this very purpose may change direction. There may arise a high resolve to discard them and mutually to give peace to the world.
>
> —Karl Jaspers[2]

A change in the "politics of aggression" must come about, but it will not come about by any objective sociopolitical process, but by a transformative change in individuals acting in unison. Although such hope is nervously present today, the conviction that the world will one day no longer know the scourge of war is not yet be found.

> How glorious, by contrast, is (this) possibility: that today . . . in this torrent of seemingly irresistible disaster, in a world where men are increasingly torn from their roots—men can meet and join in reason, love and truth.
>
> —Karl Jaspers[3]

Part Four
Meditation: Door to the
New Consciousness

The door through which we must pass to enter the new consciousness is a door that opens from the inside. No external force or "technological leap" can accomplish the task ahead. While meditation in and of itself cannot birth the new consciousness in us, without meditation it nonetheless cannot arise. Meditation is the hidden fertile ground of our rebirth, the womb and home of the Spirit.

Only meditation brings us to the discovery of the hidden jewel of the true self, the ground of our being. All spiritual traditions agree that meditation is the path to self-knowledge and the self. Christianity has marginalized the importance of meditation over recent centuries, a state of affairs that today is being gradually remedied. We are learning anew from the East.

30 ❧ The Challenge of Everyday Life

Anyone who wants to get close to God must set aside a short time each day to be with Him alone, a time of intimacy and encounter with the Lord. We must, from time to time, turn aside from our normal occupations and plunge ourselves into prayer.

—Yves Raguin[1]

In the great majority of instances, it is a truism that those who say "I can't meditate" or "I don't have time to meditate" are really saying they don't *want* to meditate, for meditation requires discipline and courage. Note that Yves Raguin, a master of the spiritual life, says we must "set aside a short time *each day* . . ." and must "*turn aside* from our normal occupations." This requires both discipline and dedication, a discipline established by the will and a dedication fired by the heart. Here the words "prayer" and "meditation" are used interchangeably. It is the "heart" that meditates, without which there is no true meditation. Thomas Merton writes: "One who really meditates also loves."

Those who understand the enormous spiritual benefits that spring from meditation and who truly wish to meditate will somehow find the will and the way, difficult as this sometimes may be. Nothing is more important. In the words of the great Teresa: "Do not let anyone deceive you by showing you a way other than prayer."

Inasmuch as Western society demands that we be practical, let us look at the person who is on the go from sunup to sundown. Perhaps this person is a mother trying to rear several young children who never cease needing care and watching and who, in the mix, may also be holding down a full- or part-time job. And what if she is a single parent with the full responsibility for children, home, and income?

It must be admitted that in such cases—more numerous than we think—prudence (one of the gifts of the Spirit) might advise against adding the practice of daily meditation periods if this would engen-

111

der strain during a certain period of one's life. Yet in such a case, if a meditation discipline could be worked into his or her busy life, that person would discover a greater and more efficient ability in dealing with duties, obligations, and attendant problems. Still, such a situation may require "waiting upon the Lord" until such time as the duties of life one day lighten up, leaving "space" for meditation. This is a personal decision, one for which a counselor should be sought. Is there an alternative?

One day a woman with a heavy daily burden of duties and obligations came to Teresa of Avila for advice, saying, try as she might, she could not find time each day to pray. Being the "both-feet-on-the-ground" kind of mystic, Teresa recommended that the woman say short prayers from time to time during her busy day and evenings. This was the method the fourth-century Desert Fathers and Mothers employed to keep themselves in the divine presence as they went about their daily tasks.

We are not monks of the fourth century whose normal routine of work was weaving baskets or tending a garden. Yet we too seek intimacy and union with God. Although we are de facto always united to God, this union needs to be made manifest. We need to know, by an experience of the heart, that we are "in Christ Jesus," an expression St. Paul used some 163 times. Only prayer/meditation can awaken our hearts to experience this truth. In so doing, our true self begins to emerge and blossom, gradually re-creating us.

Next, take the situation of someone with the "normal" round of daily duties and responsibilities and who still insists they do not have time for meditation. Thousands of others have faced this same *apparent* dilemma and, by reflectively surveying the activity of their days, have discovered they did indeed have time to meditate. We need to ask ourselves a few questions: How much time do I waste every day? How organized (or disorganized) is my day? Can I watch a half-hour less of TV without going into withdrawal? Is it necessary for me to read the daily newspaper and those magazines so thoroughly? Is it possible to go to bed a half-hour earlier so that I can rise earlier for meditation before the din of the day sets in? Can a member of the family watch the children for a half-hour each day? If my life depended on it (our spiritual life *does!*) what must I do to find that half-hour I need to survive?

If there is a genuine desire to meditate, if Love is prompting you to meditate, then Love will show you a way. It always has; it always will. That first step is the most important one, for, as St. Teresa says, it is charged with much power and grace.

When you decide to set out in search of God, you must pack your bags, saddle your horse and start on your way. But first you must say "goodbye." To whom? To what? To nothing, because the world that you are leaving will always be there, close to you, in you.

Leaving the world and self is not a matter of distance, but detachment. At all costs, you must prevent your personality from turning back on itself, from building a citadel into which you will invite God only as a guest. You must open your house and bare your heart to God.

—Yves Raguin[2]

31 ❧ Search for the True Self

The Inner self is not a part of our being; it is our entire substantial reality itself.

—Thomas Merton[1]

It is universally accepted that meditation leads to the awakening of the true or great self. Although the true self is mysterious and defies definition, it is possible to offer a few clarifying thoughts and comments. After all, a mystery is not something we know *nothing* about, but something we don't know *everything* about.

For a deeper understanding of the true self, we turn to Thomas Merton, who explored the inner self more than any Christian writer of our time, giving us profound insights into its nature, without being so foolhardy as to try to reduce it to a definition or a theological statement. To go to the essence of the matter, love is the *nature* of our true self. One can even say that love *is* our true self. Love is who we truly are; love is our identity.

Do you wish proof of this? Think about the times when you have truly, deeply loved, have gone out of yourself to become one with another. You didn't think about it at the time—for this would have ruined the whole magical experience—but, looking back, do you not now see that, in these moments, you were most truly yourself... truly the kind of person you would like to be always?

Where does this unalloyed love come from that rises up out of the depths of our being? Where does it live? Where is it to be found? Thomas Merton, an artful minister of words and a poet of the first rank, was able to bring us close to the hidden reality we refer to as the true self. "The secret of my identity," writes Merton, "is hidden in the love and mercy of God." But not in God only:

I must look for my identity, somehow, not only in God, but also in other men. I will never be able to find myself if I isolate myself from the rest of mankind as if I were a different kind of being.[2]

Just as most people are not aware they have a depth called the "unconscious," so most are unaware of their true inner selves. Only the surface waters of life are navigated; the treasures of their secret inmost depths are left undisturbed "on the bottom," relegated to becoming underwater graves for our souls. Plumbing the depths of our being and drawing up the jewel of our true self is the work of meditation, aided by grace. Our greatest teachers in this process are silence and solitude. Merton writes:

> The inner self is not a part of our being; it is our entire substantial reality itself, on its highest and most personal and most existential level. It is like life and it is life; it is our spiritual life when it is most alive.[3]

The life of which Merton speaks is none other than our *ordinary homely life* that has been rescued from illusion and ignorance. To remain in illusion and ignorance is a kind of death.

> The only true joy on earth is to escape from the prison of our own false self, and enter by love into union with the Life Who dwells and sings within the essence of every creature and in the core of our own souls.[4]

The true self never needs to defend itself or assert itself. Its "truth" is inviolable and its reality eternal. The true self does not need to defend itself because there is nothing to defend, nothing in which it is "clothed" that requires protection, because it *has* no clothes. It is lovely and pure in its kingly nakedness. The true self simply *is*—in its "suchness." The true self is beyond time and space.

If we encounter our true self, it is awakened and begins to inform us with new life, with a new spiritual vitality. No longer are our days grey and monotonous, moving from one "Spirit-less" week to the next. When the inner self is thus awakened it begins to pervade our consciousness and animate our actions, so that we become a new creation. Merton continues:

> When (the inner self) is awakened, it communicates new life to the intelligence in which it lives, so that it becomes a living awareness of itself. This awareness is not so much something that we have, as something that we are. It is a new and indefinable quality of our being.[5]

This living awareness is the experience of a higher state of consciousness, now placed in the service of our daily living and which is at our disposal during every moment of life. While this breakthrough into the inner self may suddenly "well up" as a "peak experience" (Abraham Maslow) it often develops gently and gradually, without our first noticing it. This latter kind of experience is actually the safest and the surest road back to Eden.

> Peaks come unexpectedly, suddenly they happen to us. You can't count on them. And hunting them is a little like hunting happiness. It is best not done directly.[6]

During his last two years, Maslow began to modify his view of optimal states of consciousness (peak experiences) and proposed the element of *serenity* as essential for a more lasting experience of transcendence. In contrast to the element of excitability characteristic of peak experiences, *serenity* became a distinctive component of what Maslov came to call "the plateau experience."

Our inner self is mysterious indeed, yet nonetheless real. It cannot be objectified or held under some sort of spiritual microscope to determine its constituents.

The inner self, as Merton proclaims, is "as secret as God and, like him, it evades every concept that tries to seize hold of it with full possession."

Several years ago, while I was offering a series of conferences on the Christian mystical tradition, and after speaking at some length about the true self, a woman raised her hand and asked: "But what is the true self?!" I found myself tongue-tied, realizing I had no definition to offer her. Suddenly, one of those little "lights" hit, and I asked for a copy of the Christian scriptures. Turning to St. Paul, and by making a one-word substitution in the passage I was thinking about, I was able to provide, not a definition, but a *faithful portrait* of the true self:

> The true self is always patient and kind; it is never jealous; the true self is never boastful or conceited; it is never rude or selfish; it never takes offence, and is not resentful. The true self takes no pleasure in other people's sins and faults but delights in the truth; it is always ready to

excuse, to trust, to hope, and to endure whatever comes. The true self
does not come to an end. The true self is eternal.

                                                        −1 Cor. 13:4-8

> The "I" that floats along the waves of time,
>   (from a distance I watch him)
>   With the dust and the water.
>   With the fruit and the flower,
>   With the All he is rushing forward.
>   He is always on the surface,
>   Tossed by the waves and dancing to the rhythm
>   Of Joy and suffering.
>   The least wound hurts him−
>   Him I see from afar.
>   That "I" is not my real self.
>   I am still within myself,
>   I do not float in the stream of death.
>   I am free, I am desireless,
>   I am peace, I am illumined.
>
>   −Tagore

32 ❧ Death Is Transfiguration

Because I love life, I know I shall love death.
                                    —Jalal-al-Din Rumi[1]

With a few lyrical words, Persia's greatest mystical poet lays bare the naked truth of death, as an event signifying not the end of life but an astonishing explosion of new life beyond our capacity to conceive or imagine—an adventure that will make our earthly experiences seem like ghostly phantasms. We might even say that, by contrast, the present existence we call "our life" is itself a "corridor of shadows" lived by most in darkness, where we are trapped in the world's craftily spun web of sticky illusions, stumbling along in half-conscious grey monotony day after day. Then the "resurrection moment" of death arrives, propelling us into inexpressible light, launching us upon a sea of love so all-encompassing and incredible that, were we still in our mortal bodies, we would be annihilated.

As humanity embraces the Mystical Age and is gifted in ever greater numbers with the penetrating light of higher consciousness, acceptance, peace, and serenity in the face of death will be one of the marks that this new epoch is truly under way. How unfortunate that so many people entertain a macabre fear of death, dreading even the thought or discussion of it. People put off writing their wills simply because it forces them to face the reality of death. Popular culture even offers us a cartoonish picture of death as the "grim reaper," an angular bearded old man with hollowed-out dark eyes, wielding a long scythe.

Most of us desperately hang on as if death was the end of it all, the trap door to oblivion, or something worse. Modern men and women rarely face death in a spirit of calm and serenity. Rather, we become the personification of the famous lines . . .

> Do not go gentle into that good night,
> Rage, rage against the dying of the light.

118

Animals are often wiser than are we. When an old dog or cat mysteriously knows its time has come, it calmly lies down, curls up, and, without remorse or agitation, lets go of its life. It is said that when a robin senses its end, it perches on the branch of a tree and stares into the sunset. When it can no longer see the light of the sun, it closes its eyes and falls gently to the ground. Would that we might learn from the robin, and gaze calmly, expectantly, upon the Son—raging not against the night but allowing ourselves to go gently into inexpressible light.

Psychologists tell us that those who have a tendency to procrastinate are really projecting their fear of death—their way of subconsciously trying to postpone the day when death tenaciously "digs in" on our doorstep. There is a secret voice within us that seems to echo the dying words of William Saroyan: "I know that we all must die, but I was hoping God would make an exception in my case!" There are, as well we know, no exceptions.

Death, as all the great spiritual traditions teach, is not an event to be feared but one to be awaited with a certain degree of anticipation, even joy. The mystics, as did Rumi, having experienced the glory and immortality of the human soul, have penetrated death's false disguises and have rejected the specter of death as illusory, sometimes even with contempt. Thomas Merton wrote: "I snap my fingers at death."

For the most part, Christians seem to share the same trepidation as so many others, even though scripture has given us stunningly clear assurance that death is but a transition to more abundant life: "The eye has not seen, nor the ear heard, nor has it entered into the mind of man what God has prepared for those who love him" (1 Cor. 2:9). These remain "only words" until they penetrate the heart and seep into the ground of our being. Simple intellectual faith is not sufficient to imbue us with an unshakable certitude that brings with it the gift of deep inner peace and tranquillity whenever the notion of death arises. Only those who have committed themselves to a discipline of prayer and meditation are the recipients of this reassuring gift of tranquillity in the face of death. Only the "meditator" can "hear" the Spirit give testimony to our human spirit that, because we are God's children, we are also heirs of the kingdom.

For this is what he has done: he has taken us out of the power of darkness and created a place for us in the kingdom of the Son he loves.
                                                                 —1 Cor. 13:14

As the Mystical Age proceeds, more and more of us will become
meditators in the real and profound sense of the word—meditators
whose method of practice will penetrate beyond our surface psychological selves to our true inner self, our "Christ-I," indelibly etched
with the image and likeness of God. In Christianity this practice is
called "contemplative prayer."

The five stages of grieving and dying as postulated by the
American-Swiss psychiatrist Elizabeth Kubler-Ross are identifiable
valid stages. They are, however, general postulations and not applicable to all. If one's spiritual journey has advanced to experiential union
with God, these stages will be conflated to just a few. The mystic can
easily go beyond all five stages, moving from the knowledge that
death is near to a state of joyful expectation, in the faith-knowledge
that he or she is "heading for home."

> Ah, is that not good, to shake off the earth and mortality, and to rise
> again, obtaining this boon from the Lord!
>   —Origen[2]

Out of the Buddhist tradition, the words of Tibetan Lama Sogyal
Rinpoche point to the "practice" by which calm and serenity is
attained in the face of death:

> No one can die fearlessly and in complete security until they have truly
> realized the nature of "mind." For only this realization, deepened over
> years of sustained practice can keep the mind stable during the molten
> chaos of the process of death. Of all the ways I know of helping people
> to realize the nature of "mind," that of the practice of Dzogchen, the
> most ancient and direct stream of wisdom within the teaching of
> Buddhism, is the clearest, most effective and most relevant to the needs
> of today.[3]

What, in particular, is the Dzogchen practice that can develop,
among other attributes (the flowering of virtue), an attitude of calm-
ness and serenity in the face of death, so especially needed in the
West? More importantly, is this practice relevant and accessible to the
Christian? The answer, in brief, is yes, and its counterpart is to be

found in the Christian contemplative tradition. (See part five: "Ways of Christian Contemplative Meditation.")

Merton understood that certain meditation techniques of Asia offer us "a wonderful chance of learning more about our own traditions." On the morning of his death in Bangkok, Merton closed his opening address to the First Asian Congress of Religious with the words:

> I believe that by openness to Buddhism and Hinduism, we stand a wonderful chance of learning more about our own (Christian) traditions, because they have gone, from a natural point of view, so much deeper into these things (meditation techniques) than we have.
>
> The combination of natural techniques and the graces ... that have been manifested in Asia and the Christian liberty of the Gospel should bring us all, at last, to that full and transcendent liberty which is beyond mere cultural differences and mere externals.[4]

> O Door,
> Life passes through the gateway of Death.
> At your behest, in the night of despair,
> Along the path of deliverance
> Rings the call "Fear Not."
>
> —Tagore

33 § Right Meditation

> Deep within, in the Heart of man
> there God has chosen his resting place;
> there he finds his joy.
> If only we would do that too;
> perceive those depths that lie within,
> and leaving all behind
> retire to rest therein.
>
> Yet no one ever does.
> And even so it may often be
> that a man upon his daily round
> be urged ten times, or more, to look within,
> yet still no one ever docs.
>
> —Johannes Tauler

The kingdom of God lies within. Eden awaits within. To enter the kingdom, we must make the journey inward. This means we must descend beyond the surface psychological level of consciousness and penetrate the many layers of the unconscious, where our true self awaits our discovery. This is where God "discovers himself" in us.

The discriminating mind is *the* obstacle to penetrating the deep self, which must be "naughted," or else we remain within the walled prison of our surface self, diddling around with all the flotsam that comes along on our continuous stream of consciousness. "Right meditation" means we must empty the mind of all thought, refusing to latch on to ideas, concepts, and images, which continually pop up in the mind. Our surface psychological self—our usual waking state—is the ten percent upper layer that, like the iceberg, is exposed to the atmosphere (the conscious mind). Meanwhile, a vast ocean beneath lies silent and undisturbed below the choppy waves of our exterior—the whitecaps of activity that we consciously navigate during our waking hours, the ego being our "first mate and helmsman."

During right meditation, we inform our discriminating mind to "take a hike"! The discriminating mind is rejected—all thought, all our illusions, all our accumulated knowledge and learning. Everything must be voided. Unless we do so, there can be no discovery of our true inner self. An ancient Chinese proverb says: "He who follows words (thoughts) will be destroyed!"

Because our habitual waking state is lived on the surface, it is often very difficult for us to let go of thinking, imagining, and conceptualizing—particularly those of us who have been molded by our activistic Western culture. Silence—considered by society a waste of time—does not come easily for us. It must be cultivated by a daily discipline that gradually makes us more and more comfortable with our silent, nonobjective meditation practice.

The great thirteenth-century Buddhist master Dogen taught his disciples to *"think no-thinking."* Easier said than done. However, it must also be said that there are people who are "ready for it" and take to it like a duck takes to water. It is not important how readily disposed or not we are to "right meditation"—only that we enter upon the path.

Meditation in the West is usually understood as discursive or "thinking meditation," where one develops ideas and concepts. In the East, the word "meditation" usually connotes a silent, nondiscursive practice, what we have termed "right meditation." The Christian *contemplative tradition* is rich in ways of meditation similar in form to those nonobjective meditative practices of the East. Thus Centering Prayer and Christian Mantra Prayer, traceable to the earliest Christian centuries, are being discovered anew and practiced by many thousands of Christians.

Think of yourself (*before* you go to your meditation!) as a great mountain. Clouds of all shapes and sizes (potential distractions) float endlessly by, always arriving, always departing. The mountain lets them go by without taking any notice. The mountain is unmoved. It does not allow itself to get curious about the size, shape or velocity of the clouds. *It does not discriminate.* So too when the "clouds" of thoughts/distractions come into view, we take no notice of them, but let them roll by. They come, they go. We do not allow them to descend upon us and "cloud" our meditation. We let them go. That's all—simply let them go.

A mountain remains unmoved regardless of prevailing weather conditions. It simply "sits" and allows the weather to come and go. If it's rainy, that's okay. If it's windy, that's okay too. If there is great calm and sunshine and all is serene and peaceful, that's just as okay. The mountain has trained itself not to be disturbed by whatever the atmosphere may bring. So too we must train ourselves to be detached from thoughts, reflections, lights, emotions, memories, and the like—whatever form they may take.

We must understand that irruptions of thoughts and images during our meditation period are not distractions in themselves, as we tend to think. They *become* distractions only when, upon becoming aware of their presence, we *willfully* and *intentionally* latch on to them and develop them. To return to the metaphor of the stream of consciousness, it is only when we follow these thoughts downstream that they become distractions. Otherwise, they are simply clouds that harmlessly come and go—noticed, but not adhered to.

Thus, it is important that we train ourselves in *detachment*, a necessary quality (almost a virtue!) in meditation. God loves a heart that is detached from whatever is not God, that turns from everything else and listens to God in silence. No matter how many thoughts, images, and memories cascade down upon us, by ignoring them, a simple undifferentiated awareness remains; a disposition of active receptivity continues. We are a mountain that cannot be moved. If, however, we *consciously* and *deliberately* allow ourselves to become attached to a thought or image, then we have allowed the mountain to be moved. There is only one remedy—gently, calmly bring yourself back to your meditation.

As we are drawn deeper into meditation and states of absorption, the false ego-I begins to subside and dissolve in the great reality of the true self, where the living God sings and dwells. At a certain depth level, duality vanishes and is subsumed in the darkness and obscurity of our mysterious inner self. The I-Thou relationship (Buber) dissolves into oneness. Although two are involved, the experience is "not two."

Don't dream this thread is double-ply:
root and branch are but One.
Look close: all is He—
but He is manifest through me.

—Fahkruddin ʿIraqi

As the discriminating mind is brought under control and temporarily "naughted," God is accessed and held close by love, grounded in faith. We are given a loving knowledge of God that transcends all boundaries of thought and concepts. The "heart" takes over and becomes the "living conduit" of our love of God and God's tremendous love for us. "He may well be loved," reminds the author of *The Cloud of Unknowing*, "but he cannot be thought. He may well be held close by love, but never by thought."[1]

In silent, wordless communion with Christ in God, the words of St. Paul become our own experience: "Anyone who is joined to the Lord, is one spirit with him" (1 Cor. 6:17). Shutting down the discriminating mind applies only to our formal meditation periods. Our intellectual faculties return once we have left our meditation and serve us with renewed energy and light. Otherwise we would all be walking around like zombies, bumping into walls and tripping over whatever is in front of us!

Lectio Divina, the prayerful reading of scripture, is a most important nourishment for the spiritual journey, just as food is essential for physical health. The spiritual nutrients received are part of the preparation for meditation itself. Again, there are vast numbers of people who do not meditate, who dismiss meditation as unimportant, or who cite lack of time as their reason—not wanting to make the effort to undertake the inward journey. One year follows the next; they live exclusively on the psychological sense/surface level of awareness. Karl Rahner describes their situation, words which could be chiseled on their tombstones:

Our soul seems to continue its weary way on the road, followed endlessly by the multitude of its innumerable trifles, its gossip, its pretence, its curiosity and vanity. One day after the other we go on like this to the hour of our death, when all the goods and chattels which we called "our life" will be swept away. What will we be then? What will remain of us, whose life was nothing but the business of the day, of idle talk and vain pretence?[2]

Nothing is more vital, more life-nurturing, than to penetrate "our Mystery" and "our Deep" and to come to know our true inner self—not by some process of the intellect but by a direct intuitive experience. During the time we enter "the Deep," we are in the fourth spiritual dimension, enlightened by "the truth that sets us free." True inner freedom, spontaneity, and authenticity are among the gifts of the inner self. This experience is beyond time and space; it is an experience of the fourth spiritual dimension, an experience of the *eternal now.*

> Time and space are fragments,
> but God is one.
> Should man then recognize God,
> he must recognize him beyond
> time and space;
> for God is neither this nor that
> like these earthly multifarious things;
> for God is one.
>   —Meister Eckhart

34 ❦ Right Understanding

> If you and I are to further the evolution of mankind . . . if we are to contribute to evolution and not merely siphon it off . . . if we are to help the overcoming of our self-alienation from the Spirit and not merely perpetuate it, then meditation—or a similar and truly contemplative practice—becomes an absolute ethical imperative.
>
> —Ken Wilber[1]

As truly meaningful contact and dialogue with Eastern spiritual traditions have emerged over the latter part of the twentieth century, Western Christianity has been awakened and enriched by knowledge of certain Eastern meditation practices. It has, first of all, been awakened to its own contemplative meditation/prayer tradition going back to the earliest Christian centuries. It has been enriched by those who have undertaken training in such Eastern practices as Zen meditation. Since Zen is not a religion, Christians, under experienced tutelage, have been able to fruitfully integrate Zen meditation practices into their spiritual journey.

Two of several notable Christians who have undergone extensive training in these schools are the Jesuits William Johnston and Hugo Enomiya-Lassalle. Not only did they remain committed Christians, but they emerged *better* Christians for the experience. The Austrian-born Benedictine mystic David Steindl-Rast, who has studied with several Zen Roshis, once asked Merton if he could have presented the Christian teaching in the deeper way that Merton did without his exposure to Buddhism. After a time of reflection, Merton replied: "You know, I thought about your question, and I think I couldn't understand Christian teaching the way I do if it were not in the light of Buddhism."

The aim of both Eastern and Christian contemplative ways of non-objective meditation is to lead the meditator beyond the surface "small self" and penetrate the vast interior sea of the unconscious, the cave dwelling of the great or true self. Entering into the deep self, into the ground of one's being, is, in Christianity, the gateway to the indwelling divine life.

> In Christianity, the inner self is a stepping stone to an awareness of God. Man is the image of God, and his inner self is a kind of mirror in which God is reflected. Thus, through the dark, transparent mystery of our own inner being we can, as it were, see God "through a glass darkly."
>
> All this, of course, is pure metaphor. It is a way of saying that our being somehow communicates directly with the Being of God, Who is in us. If we enter into ourselves and find our true self, and then pass "beyond" the inner "I", we sail forth into the immense darkness in which we confront the I AM of the Almighty.
>
> Our awareness of God is a supernatural participation in the light by which God reveals himself interiorly as dwelling in our inmost self. The Christian mystical experience is not only an awareness of the inner self, but also, by a supernatural intensification of faith, it is an experiential grasp of God as present within our inner self. Here we come upon one of the distinctive features of Christian, Jewish and Islamic mysticisms.
>
> —Thomas Merton[2]

This experiential encounter with God is an awareness of the divine incomprehensibility. In darkness, we "see"; in unknowing, we "know." Merton points out that this "confrontation with the Almighty" is a unitive experience in which God becomes, so to speak, *subjective*. All that different forms of nonobjective meditation can accomplish is to till the soil of our inner being and prepare it to receive the seeds of enlightenment—for the Christian, the seeds of *infused contemplation*. Enlightenment, as the East understands and experiences it, is impersonal. For the Christian, the experience of infused contemplation is a profoundly personal encounter. Saying this sounds dualistic. The *experience*, however, is unitive.

Discursive prayer, inasmuch as it operates on the surface psychological level, cannot encounter (experience) God, regardless of whatever "feelings and emotions" (psychological level) might suggest. Discursive or reasoning prayer/meditation is "active" and functions purely on the psychological level. As such it is the ego that leads the way and secretly directs all its maneuvering. The mystical experience of God has nothing to do with feelings or emotions, although the encounter will at times overflow into the senses. As long as prayer/meditation remains on the psychological level, our efforts (here *we* set the agenda) are defiled by the encroachment of the false exterior self:

> So far as our spiritual life consists of thoughts, desires, actions, devotions and projects of our exterior self, it participates in the non-being and exterior falsity of that exterior self.
>
> —Thomas Merton[3]

To stay forever with mental, discursive prayer/meditation is to remain on the "outskirts" of the kingdom of God, which is *within*. To stay with discursive ways means that one will never deeply experience God. Being an "out-skirter" also runs the hazard of becoming an "outcast" when life gets rough and the storms of life threaten to engulf us. Unless our roots run deep, we run the terrible risk of our spirituality being completely blown away.

At the same time it should be noted that discursive ways of prayer should not be demeaned or "put down," for these plodding steps of word-prayer may one day take wings:

> Today there is a reaction to discursive prayer. Yet this is a good, solid form of prayer. Many people have begun with discursive prayer and wound up consummate mystics. The path traced out by mystical theologians—discursive prayer to contemplation—is very valuable, provided we do not consider it a road everyone must travel.
>
> —William Johnston[4]

A danger lies in wait, however, for the neophyte inexperienced in the ways of nonobjective contemplative prayer, and it is this: Having heard that nonobjective or contemplative prayer is a higher, more perfect way, he or she—subtly moved by the ego—forays into this uncharted territory and soon encounters pitfalls and difficulties of all kinds. In time, this can foster disillusionment and discouragement, causing the neophytes to throw up their hands and give up the practice.

As Basil Pennington writes in *Centering Prayer*, "we must be ready for it." Being ready implies having, in most cases, an experienced teacher—at least in the initial phases—and, second, having a basic understanding of the psychological aspects of contemplative prayer. These include foreknowledge of the Night of Sense, an understanding

of how to deal with emptiness and darkness, as well as some understanding of the psychological process involved in the eventual unloading of the unconscious. These areas are treated in later chapters.
*No one comes to the experiential knowledge of God except in
silence and in darkness*—when the discriminating mind is "voided"
and the inferior parts of the intellect—memory and imagination—are
barred from entrance. In the East, the death of the discriminating
mind is the essential prerequisite for enlightenment. In Christianity,
it is the prerequisite for receiving the seeds of infused contemplation, the greatest gift God can bestow on earth—a foretaste, though
but a small morsel, of heaven. We can liken this death of the discriminating mind to the death of the false exterior self inasmuch as
it implies a letting go of all attachments and all forms of self-seeking
and self-aggrandizement. It can thus be likened to the sixth beatitude: "Happy are those who are pure of heart, for they shall see
God." In Christianity the fulfillment of this promise is what we know
as contemplation.

> As far as possible, raise thyself up in unknowing, even unto union with
> Him Who is beyond all essence and all knowledge, for it is indeed by
> going out of thyself . . . free and pure, that thou shalt raise thyself up to
> the pure and superessential ray of the divine darkness.
> —Pseudo Dionysius[5]

35   Right Attitude

> To gaze with utterly purified eyes on the divinity is possible—but only
> to those who rise above lowly and earthly works and thoughts and who
> retreat with Him into the high mountains of solitude . . . and when they
> are freed from the tumult of worldly ideas and passions.
>
> —John Cassian[1]

Inner attitude is important in all forms of nonobjective "right meditation." Without "right attitude," our meditation efforts will fail. Like
the cork on a fishing line that continually bobs up to the surface
whenever fish nibble on the bait, so will we mostly bob around on the
surface without right attitude—when thoughts and images nibble at
us. For most, the descent into "the Deep" is a very gradual process—
like being enclosed in the solitude of a diving bell and lowered ever
so gradually into the deep. The depths take getting used to. These are
new waters, and it usually takes time, practice, patience, and fortitude—until we become adjusted to the darkness and silence that is
the hushed habitat of our true self.

Whether one sits in the lotus position, the half-lotus position, or
sits in a straight-backed chair, we must bring ourselves to a relaxed
state of simple awareness. When we say "simple," we mean not being
aware of our awareness, not reflecting on it, not thinking that we are
being aware. To say this another way, we do not watch ourselves
being aware. To do so would be another, subtler activity of the discriminating mind. We would still be bobbing around on the surface
waves of our exterior self. Right attitude means letting go of every
form of consciousness, including the consciousness of being aware
that we are aware!

Another way to express right attitude is *active receptivity*. The
active aspect is being alert; the receptivity aspect is being open and
passive, letting go of our discriminating mind and allowing ourselves

to simply "be." This is not to suggest that we sit like a bump on a log, blank out and go stupid! In Christianity, this would be to succumb to the seventeenth-century heresy of Quietism, which was a treadmill to no-man's-land, leading not to life but to a kind of stagnation and spiritual death. We are meant to become fully alive people, not lifeless cadavers. "I have come that you might have joy, and have it to the full" (John 16:24).

Something else must be said relating to right attitude, concerning the disposition of mind that we bring to our meditation. The Desert Father John Cassian, who brought the spiritual teachings of the fourth-century Egyptian Desert Fathers to the West, teaches that the disposition of mind and heart that we wish to have during our meditation period should be in place before we come to our formal meditation.

> In advance of prayer we must strive to dispose ourselves as we would wish to be during prayer. The "praying spirit" is shaped by its earlier condition.
>
> —John Cassian[2]

Whatever our mental and psychological state is prior to our meditation will be carried over *into* our meditation. We must strive to attain a serene and centered state of consciousness prior to our meditation, which, when entered, will deepen and expand. How can this be achieved?

First of all, it should be obvious that if we fritter away the previous hours and days in idle talk, in unrestrained mental wanderings, in throwing ourselves into useless activities, then our meditation will suffer the "slings and arrows" of our outrageous behavior. To allow our imagination to run riot, to indulge ourselves in day-dreaming and fantasizing, to spend our day chewing over the past and projecting into an unknown future—all this clutter will enter our meditation and mercilessly pepper us with its fallout.

A "spirit of recollection" needs to be cultivated during those hours outside of our formal prayer times. The best way to achieve this is the way taught by the Desert Fathers—by quiet, gentle, interior recitation of short prayers (aspirations) from time to time as we go throughout the day (like beads that follow one another on a string of pearls, the string representing the length of our days). Let us remember that recollection takes *two*: ourselves, and the Holy Spirit.

This way of interiorly reciting short "mantras" is appropriate even when (especially when) we are engaged in work that is demanding of our mental faculties and concentration. There are always moments when we can stop, take a breath, and bring ourselves back, at least momentarily, to the presence of God by use of a short prayer, of which there can be an infinite variety. The "Jesus Prayer" was such a prayer used by the Desert Fathers to keep themselves recollected and aware of God's presence. (See chapter 37: "The Way of the Jesus Prayer.")

Cassian taught that the spirit of a person detached from worldly allurements and involvements would, on its own, rise effortlessly, like a "dry feather" to God at the time of prayer.

> The soul may be quite sensibly compared to the finest down and the lightest feather which, if spared the onset and penetration of dampness without, have a nature so mobile that, at the slightest breeze, they rise up of themselves to the highest points of the sky.
>
> So too with our soul. If sin and worldly preoccupation have not weighed it down, if dangerous passion has not sullied it, then lifted up by the natural goodness of its purity, it will rise to the heights on the lightest breath of meditation, and leaving the lowly things, it will travel upward to the heavenly and invisible.
>
> —John Cassian[3]

Meditation should be effortless, without struggle, devoid of an attitude of "trying to attain," what can be called "egoic effort." The more we insert ourselves through egoic effort, the more the false ego-I blocks the free flow of grace. We do not have to strive; we have simply to be open so as to receive fully. We surrender our entire being into the hands of Another. In this attitude we are no longer the seeker but the receiver. True meditation is simply witnessing. Witnessing what? In darkness and obscurity we witness the divine indwelling. God's work is to create us new beings. Our work is simply to receive the gift.

> When a contemplative person has attained His eternal image, and in this purity and by means of the Son has possessed the Father's bosom, then he is enlightened with divine truth. Here arises the last point,

which is a meeting in love. It is in this more than anything else that our highest blessedness resides.

—John Ruysbroeck[4]

By way of concluding this chapter, it should be said that the way of nonobjective meditation is *not* a narcissistic form of introspection (one of the pitfalls of the New Age movement). Such "navel gazing" is the worst kind of trap, for it encloses one in the prison of the false empirical self, the self that can be seen and objectified. This exterior self must be transcended and left behind. In Christianity, the experience of encountering our deep true self is an encounter with our inner "Christ-I," the source and ground of our being. To so experience is to be enlightened—to come to the realization that the self we thought ourselves to be is an illusion. To see our false exterior self as illusion, and therefore unreal, is to rejoice in what truly really *is*.

One day Yen Kwai approached his master, Confucius and said "I am making progress."

"What do you mean by that?" asked Confucius.

"I can sit in oblivion" replied Yen Kwai.

"What do you mean by that?" asked Confucius.

"I let my limbs and body drop away, dry up my intellect, cast off all forms, do away with understanding, and make myself identical with the Tao.

"This is what I mean when I say 'I sit in oblivion.'"

Confucius then asked to become Yen Kwai's disciple instead.

Part Five
Ways of Christian
Contemplative Meditation

Although meditation in and of itself cannot induce the higher consciousness, nonetheless, without meditation the new mutation will not unfold within the individual. While there are many forms/methods of non-objective meditation, all should eventually "empty out" into a simple on-going awareness and abiding consciousness of God, which should deepen over time:

"At a certain level when one leaves the psychic realm in which the spirit is active, all movement (employment of methods) come to an end, and even prayer itself ceases. This is the perfecting of prayer, and is called spiritual prayer, or contemplation." [1]

Thomas Keating writes what can be applied to all methods of non-objective meditation: *"It reduces the obstacles to the Gifts of the Spirit. It really ceases to be (a method) and becomes whatever the Spirit leads people to, as the gift of Wisdom unfolds."* [2]

Those who are able to enclose themselves within the heaven of their soul ... and grow accustomed to refusing to go where their distractions would lead them ... can be sure they are travelling by a most excellent way, for they will travel far in a short time; and they will not fail to drink of the living water from the fount of contemplation.

—Teresa of Avila[3]

36 ❧ The Way of the Mantra

> The soul must grasp onto a short phrase, so that saying it over and over again . . . it has the strength to reject and refuse all the abundant riches of thought.
>
> —John Cassian[1]

The fourth-century Desert Fathers understood that a simple device was needed to keep the "monkey mind" from wandering and going off on mental excursions that would draw them out of the presence of God. They would select a short verse from scripture and calmly, interiorly repeat the verse (mantra) during those times when they were not engaged in the work of God (*Opus Dei*), the praying/chanting of the Psalms. Cassian writes:

> Hence our need to find a formula which will enable us to think of God and to hold incessantly to that single thought . . . so that we will have something to immediately return to whenever we have somehow slipped away from it.
>
> —John Cassian[2]

Thus, the mantra method of prayer, which had been introduced centuries before by Buddhists and Hindus, came to be a stable form of Christian prayer, not only for the Desert Fathers and Mothers but for Christians down through the ages.

> The mantra is a powerful tool for quieting the mind during the process of meditation. Not only can you use the mantra for the formal practice of meditation, but it can also be repeated silently as you go about your daily activities.
>
> —Swami Muktananda[3]

As Christianity moved into the Middle Ages, the way of the mantra prayer was largely discarded. During the mid-1970s, this ancient and authentic method of Christian prayer was rescued from the dusty archives of the Church's treasures by the Benedictine John Main, then prior of the Benedictine Priory in Montreal. The priory became not only a center for worldwide fellowship of prayer, but the dynamic hub from which the spokes of the mantra method would radiate out to the world.

The mantra method is utterly simple (do not confuse "simple" with "easy"!). During formal meditation periods, our chosen mantra verse is calmly, serenely repeated over the time allotted. It should be unrushed and a "space" opened up before each repetition–perhaps as long as it takes to actually pray the verse. This empty space is important, for it allows the inclusion of the most important aspect of all prayer forms–*listening*–listening to the Spirit who speaks silently, profoundly, and mysteriously to us in the deepest depths of our heart. There are no words–only the Word.

Having once chosen a short verse from scripture as our mantra prayer, we may or may not continue with that same verse indefinitely. We certainly can hold to it indefinitely if we wish and feel comfortable doing so, as do those who follow the way of the Jesus Prayer. On the other hand, if we feel we would like to introduce another short passage from scripture as our mantra prayer, we are free to do so. The Spirit will guide us in such matters.

John Main enumerates three preliminary aims of the way of the mantra:

> The first is simply to say the mantra for the full duration of the meditation. It will probably take some time to achieve this first stage, and we will have to learn patience in the meantime. We cannot force anything . . . but must simply say the mantra without haste or expectation.
>
> The second aim is to say the mantra throughout the meditation without interruption, while remaining quite calm in the face of all distractions.
>
> The third aim is to say the mantra for the entire time of the meditation quite free of all distractions. The surface areas of the mind are now in tune with the deep peacefulness at the core of our being. In this state we have passed beyond thought, beyond imagination, and beyond all images. We simply rest with the Reality, the realized presence of God dwelling within our hearts.[4]

THE PRACTICE

John Main summarizes the practice of the Christian mantra thusly:

> Begin by sitting down comfortably and calmly and then start to say your mantra in the silence of your mind. Repeat the mantra calmly, serenely for the full time of your meditation, that is for about twenty to thirty minutes.
>
> We begin by saying the mantra in the mind. For modern Westerners who have so restricted themselves to the mental modality, there is no other way to begin. But as we progress with simple fidelity, the mantra begins to sound not so much in our head but rather in the heart. That is, it seems to become rooted in the very depths of our being.[5]

Two short books are recommended to the reader, both by John Main:

Word Into Silence. Ramsey, N.J.: Paulist Press, 1980
The Way of Unknowing. New York: Crossroad, 1990.

37 ❦ The Way of the Jesus Prayer

Lord, Jesus Christ, Son of God, have mercy on me, a sinner.

The Jesus Prayer has been rightly called "the great Christian mantra." It is the gift of the Eastern church to the West and evolved out of the desert experience of the fourth-century Hesychast Fathers (hesychast = tranquillity), who made this mantra prayer a way of life. Its practice is rooted in an integral, holistic view of the human person, leading to the transformation of body, soul, and spirit. Its present form is traceable to the sixth century in Sinai.

An aim of the Jesus Prayer is to achieve "one-pointedness," to reduce the stream of multiple thoughts to a single point, *the person of Jesus,* induced by the repetition of the Holy Name. In the fifth century, Bishop Diadochus of Pholike proposed that a specific task be given the mind to occupy it while at the same time not allowing it to become too active. He proposed the repetition of the Jesus Prayer.

The Jesus Prayer is more than simply a way of inducing inner peace and tranquillity. The Holy Name stands for the glorified person of Jesus, the recitation of whose name is quasi-sacramental, rendering Jesus present. The practitioner is drawn to embrace the Lord and to experience his presence in the heart and his saving power (the diminution of the false self). Thus the practice came to be known as "prayer of the heart." What is the biblical concept of "the heart"?

> The heart is the innermost person, or spirit. Here are located self-awareness, the conscience, the idea of God ... and all the treasures of the spiritual life. Stand in the heart, with the faith that God is also there, but how he is there do not speculate.
>
> —Theophane the Recluse[1]

The heart, writes George A. Maloney, is "where I take my life in hand," and Thomas Merton alludes to the heart when he writes:

There exists some point at which I can meet God in a real and experiential contact with his infinite actuality. This is the "place" of God, his sanctuary. It is the point where my contingent being depends upon his love.[2]

Pseudo-Macarius gives us a beautiful and holistic concept of the heart:

Divine grace writes on the tables of the heart the laws of the spirit and the heavenly mysteries. For the heart directs and governs all the organs of the body. When grace enters the heart, it rules over all the bodily members and the thoughts of the soul and all its hopes.[3]

In terms of modern psychology, the heart may be considered to be the unconscious, personal or collective. The heart, then, is the point of transcendence where we meet God in his infinite actuality and, as a consequence, are saved, that is, transformed.

A somewhat complex psycho-physiological method of the Jesus Prayer was developed by the monks of Mt. Athos in the fourteenth century. The method involved a sitting posture, head bent (chin touching the chest), practicing certain breathing techniques, and interiorly gazing at the center of one's belly in search of the "place of the heart." (It is interesting that in Taoism and Confucianism, this "center of the spirit" is thought to be situated about two inches below and two inches behind the navel.) Many contemporary Orthodox writers, however, lay much less emphasis on these external methods, teaching that such physical and breathing methods are *not essential* to the efficacy of the prayer.

One of the greatest teachers of the Jesus Prayer, St. Theophane the Recluse of nineteenth-century Russia, took care to drop out of the *Philokalia* those writings that too heavily stressed the physical techniques.[4] Theophane adds:

The descent of the mind into the heart by the way of breathing is suggested in the case of anyone who does not know where to hold his attention, or where the heart is; but if you know how to find the heart without this method, then choose your own way there.[5]

Another great teacher of early nineteenth-century Russia, Bishop Brianchaninov, advises to look to the "simplest and humblest of aids, since they are the safest." In Greek, the Jesus Prayer is only eight words. Its twelve-word English translation makes it somewhat lengthy, and many use a shortened form, such as: "Lord Jesus Christ, have mercy," or simply, "Jesus mercy." What is important is that the prayer be centered, in faith, on the name of Jesus.

While the repetition of the Jesus Prayer many hundreds, even thousands of times a day may be appropriate for monks of Mt. Athos, such is not recommended for the rest of us. This way of practicing the Jesus Prayer will not work for Americans!

> I think it is all very well for a nineteenth century Russian monk to do that all day and night, but it is not going to work for Americans. As for the breathing, I would get some idea of some good Yoga breathing and use that sometimes. If a simple ejaculation helps, well and good. Words do not always help. Just looking is often more helpful.
> — *Thomas Merton* ~~Brianchaninov~~[6]

The Western psyche is not culturally formed and conditioned in the same mode as the Eastern European psyche. One cannot simply overlay the historical method of the practice of the Jesus Prayer on Westerners without making certain modifications and adjustments. The practice of the Jesus Prayer is certainly suitable for a twenty- or thirty-minute meditation period, repeated calmly and unhurriedly. One who practices the Prayer this way can forgo the injunction of Orthodoxy that the practice of the Jesus Prayer should be undertaken only under the guidance of a spiritual director so as to avoid undesirable psychological consequences.

In truth, *any* mantra repeated many hundreds or thousands of times will produce certain adverse psychological effects, including mind-altering and possible delusionary states. The Jesus Prayer, practiced for short periods of time, serenely and unrushed, does not run such risks and needs only one "director"—the indwelling Holy Spirit.

There are three developmental stages of the Jesus Prayer. One of the great modern Orthodox theologians, Bishop Kallistos Ware, writes:

> To begin with, The Jesus Prayer is an oral prayer like any other: the words are prayed aloud, or at least formed silently on the lips. During

this initial stage, the attentive repetition of the Prayer often proves a hard ... calling for humble persistence.

In the course of time, the Prayer becomes more inward, and the mind repeats it without any outward movement of lips or tongue. The concentration also becomes easier. The Prayer gradually acquires a rhythm of its own.

Finally, the Prayer enters the heart, dominating the entire personality. Its rhythm is identified more and more closely with the rhythm of the heart, until it finally becomes unceasing.[7]

Upon entering the heart and becoming stable there, the Jesus Prayer begins to "pray itself" under the influence of the Holy Spirit, thus fulfilling the injunction of St. Paul to "pray incessantly" (1 Thess. 5:17). In the words of a great Russian staretz of Mt. Athos, the Jesus Prayer becomes a "murmuring stream within the heart," continuing to flow unceasingly.

THE PRACTICE

The Jesus Prayer is first repeated softly aloud again and again. This may be looked upon as the conditioning of the body. When this has been practiced for some time, the next step is taken, which is to say the prayer silently. This might be looked upon as the conditioning of the mind. Again and again the mind must be brought back to the prayer until one realizes that the mind is indeed like a wagon full of monkeys.

The third step, when complete concentration has been attained, is then taken. The Prayer enters the heart and lives itself with every heart beat. The direct link is created between body and spirit and the "divine intermediary" of the soul is dispensed with.

—Brianchaninov[8]

Recommended reading: *The Jesus Prayer by a Monk of the Orthodox Church* (Crestwood, N.Y.: St. Vladimir Press, 1995).

38 🌸 The Way of Centering Prayer

> When you first begin to undertake this practice, you will find it is dark-
> ness, a sort of cloud of unknowing. You cannot tell what it is, except
> that you experience in your will a simple reaching out for God.
> —*The Cloud of Unknowing*[1]

At about the same time that the Benedictine John Main was reviving
the practice of the Christian mantra, Trappist Thomas Keating, then
Abbot of St. Joseph Monastery in Massachusetts, was developing,
with some brother monks, the Way of Centering Prayer, a prayer form
rooted in the fourteenth-century English classic *The Cloud of
Unknowing*. This form of silent, listening prayer is also traceable to
the fourth century and has been known by other names in other
times: the Prayer of Simplicity, the Prayer of Silence, the Prayer of
Inward Gaze, the Prayer of Recollection.

Centering Prayer employs what is called a "sacred word" (Basil
Pennington calls it his "prayer word"), which is silently evoked whenever we find ourselves caught up in a thought (distraction) that
threatens to absorb us, taking us away from our "one-pointedness."

> Take just a little word . . . one which you prefer. This word will be your
> shield and your spear. With this word, you are to strike down every
> kind of thought under the cloud of forgetting.
> —*The Cloud of Unknowing*[2]

In his introduction to *Open Mind, Open Heart,* Thomas Keating
explains the rationale behind the way of Centering Prayer:

> Centering Prayer is an effort to renew the teaching of the Christian tra-
> dition on contemplative prayer. It is an attempt to present that tradition
> in an up-to-date form and to put a certain order and method into it. Like
> the word contemplation, the term centering prayer has come to have a
> variety of meanings.
> For the sake of clarity, it seems best to reserve the term centering
> prayer for the specific method of preparing for the gift of contempla-

tion, and to return to the traditional term contemplative prayer when describing its development under the more direct inspiration of the Spirit.[3]

Centering Prayer's "sacred word" is not a mantra that is deliberately and conscientiously repeated over and over again, whether or not we have become caught up in a particular thought. The sacred word is brought into play *only* when we become aware that a thought-image-idea has caught our attention and is "inviting us in." Such thoughts, like sticky glue, require a "glue dissolver" (the sacred word) so we can remove ourselves from the "thought of the moment," of which there will be many. The sacred word simply *renews our intention* to be in God's presence.

The sacred word is not a "holy" word or necessarily a word from scripture. It can be any one- or two-syllable word of our choice that we find comfortable: *Peace, quiet, silence, joy, hope, love* are all words that can be chosen—or *Jesus, Lord, Abba, Father, Spirit.* The sacred word is simply sacred to *us.*

As the stream of consciousness continuously meanders on, we discover how easily we are caught up by a thought or image and invited to browse around. Like the tractor beams in the *Star Trek* television series, we are pulled in their direction. The sacred word is our "release mechanism" for disengaging ourselves.

At this moment, our training in the use of the sacred word comes to the rescue and we renew our intention to open ourselves to God's presence and action in us. *Centering Prayer has more to do with intention than attention.* The heart of Centering Prayer is our intention to be open to God's presence and action, an intention that is renewed each time we evoke our sacred word.

As Thomas Keating has said, "The sacred word doesn't work very well!" In other words, the stream of consciousness that wants to carry us downstream cannot be emptied out into some ocean, it can only be slowed. The sacred word opens up little spaces until the next thought arises in our consciousness and we begin the discipline all over again. By using the sacred word we cut off the incessant interior dialogue that goes on within us from the moment we awake until we fall asleep, and which continues on in the dream state.

THE PRACTICE

As with all meditation times, we should choose a prime time when we are alert and "with it." We enter our private place and take a comfortable position. For most people this is a sitting position on a straight-backed chair (not a Stratolounger!) feet on the floor and hands gently clasped on one's lap. Zen practitioners recommend that the thumbs touch, to complete a circle of energy.

We have, beforehand, already chosen our sacred word—the symbol of our intent to be in the presence of God and open to his action in us. To begin, we gently introduce our sacred word and return to it when—and *only* when—we become aware that a thought has caught our attention. This process continues throughout our meditation period. Thus, it is not a mantra form of prayer, which is conscientiously and deliberately repeated over and over again regardless of whether or not one has become aware of a thought or image.

Thomas Keating recommends that we devote two twenty-minute periods daily to our Centering Prayer practice. This is not always possible for people who must deal with a myriad of duties and obligations throughout the day. In such a case, we should meditate for one twenty-minute period until circumstances permit us to devote two such periods a day.

The "bible" of the way of Centering Prayer is Thomas Keating's *Open Mind, Open Heart* (New York: Continuum, 1995). Also valuable is his *Intimacy With God* (New York: Crossroad, 1994); and Basil Pennington's *Centering Prayer* (New York: Image Books, 1982).

39 ❦ The Way of Zen

Better to see the face than to hear the name.

—Zen saying

Zen is a way of discovering the true self. Although Zen meditation comes out of the Buddhist experience, it is not religious in the sense that it is tied to any one spiritual path. To say this differently: If Zen is undertaken by a Buddhist, it becomes a Buddhist way. When undertaken by a Christian, it is a Christian way. Zen does not discriminate! The great thirteenth-century Zen Master Dogen said: "Anyone who would regard Zen as a school or as a sect of Buddhism . . . is a devil!"[1] Thus, Zen has appeal to Christians as well as to those who follow Eastern paths. Let it also be said that Zen has no structure, no shape or form. There is nothing to be understood; there is nothing to be seen. Merton writes:

> To define Zen in terms of a religious system of structure is in fact to destroy it—or rather, to miss it completely.[2]

Neither should we Westerners romantically think of Zen as mysterious or esoteric or exotic. It is simply *Zen*. Let's not make the mistake of messing with it!

> Buddhist meditation, and above all that of Zen, seeks not to explain anything, but to pay attention, to become aware, to be mindful—in other words to develop a certain kind of consciousness that is above and beyond deception by certain formulas, or by emotional excitement.
>
> —Thomas Merton[3]

One day someone asked the Buddha: "Are you a god?" The Buddha answered, "No, I am not a god." He was then asked, "Are you a magician?" "No," replied the Buddha, "I am not a magician." "Then what are you?" asked the questioner. "I am awake!" A buddha is one who, having attained enlightenment, is awake. Merton depicts Zen as "an alarm clock ringing."

147

In this chapter we will omit the teaching on the "way of the koan" (the Rinzai school of Zen) and direct our observations to two other aspects of Zen, the "way of Zazen," or sitting meditation (Soto school), and the "way of the breath." We will also omit the prescriptions of working with a master, something that is of primary importance to Buddhists in Zen practice. It is said that enlightenment is not transmitted by words or teachings, but through *ishin-denshin*, from heart to heart, from master to disciple. Here again, for the Christian, the indwelling Holy Spirit is our "guru and master" and will "transmit" her hidden treasures. This is not to dismiss the great value of having a spiritual guide.

In Zazen, our eyes remain slightly open and "gazing" on a point on the floor about two to three feet away from our sitting position. Keeping the eyes slightly open is said to prevent mental images from appearing on the "screen of our mind." This instruction is helpful but not foolproof. However, if we close our eyes, it can no longer be considered the Way of Zen. If we close our eyes, we are moving into the way of Centering Prayer.

Like other forms of nonobjective meditation, breathing is important, just as inner attitude is important. Breathing should be from the diaphragm, unforced, and should flow naturally. It is recommended that when starting out, we concentrate on our breath, counting each breath from one to ten and then starting over again. At some point we may let go and "simply sit" (the meaning of Zazen). The Desert Fathers had a saying: "Stay in your cell and it will teach you everything." Silence is the great teacher. Simply sitting in silence, in awareness—this is our "cell" that will teach us everything. Teach us what? Teach us to be silent. Teach us to be empty (*sunyata*) so that we may be filled. In Christianity, this is the work of grace.

Meister Eckhart said that he never prayed for God to fill him—he prayed that God would empty him. "Then," said Eckhart, "God will be obliged to fill me with himself." As with all nonobjective forms of meditation, the difficulty is letting go of all thoughts, of all images, of all thinking. In the final stage, we come to stillness, we "open out" into emptiness.

As Eckhart said: "Get out of the way and let God be God in you!" The more we tinker with thoughts and ideas and the theology of it all, the more we destroy the efficacy of meditation—the more we send ourselves down the disheartening road to defeat.

> The way to enlightenment is a way of purification. There are no short-cuts and (when working with a master) one will not be allowed to fool oneself for the sake of personal convenience. At various points along the way there will be times when one is forced to face painful realizations about oneself.
>
> —Enomiya-Lassalle[4]

It is salutary—perhaps essential—for a Christian to learn about the Way of Zen from a Zen master who is also a Christian.

The following book is the best known to me in this regard:
Hugo M. Enomiya-Lassalle, S.J. *The Practice of Zen Meditation.* San Francisco: Aquarian Press, 1990.

40   The Way of the Breath

Our true home is in the present moment. To live in the present moment is a miracle. The miracle is not to walk on water—the miracle is to walk on the green Earth in the present moment, to appreciate the peace and beauty that is available now. Once we learn to touch this peace, we will be healed and transformed.

—Thich Naht Hanh[1]

The practice of being aware of one's breath is a way of becoming centered, of becoming mindful, of touching peace. Synchronizing one's breath with a meditation practice is not unknown in the Christian contemplative tradition, going back to the hesychast Desert Fathers and their practice of the Jesus Prayer. Practitioners of the Jesus Prayer usually have started out by unhurriedly breathing in—"Lord Jesus Christ, Son of God"—and exhaling—"Have mercy on me, a sinner." In time, the breathing practice is discontinued (it "falls away" on its own). The way of a meditation practice that involves watching or counting one's breath exclusively, however, comes out of the Buddhist tradition, going back to when the Buddha gave his teaching on the Full Awareness of Breathing. This teaching had its roots in earlier Yoga-Upanishadic meditation systems.

Like the Way of Zen, the Way of the Breath is devoid of any Buddhist, Hindu, or other religious content and takes the "formless form" of the intention of the practitioner. Thus a Christian may feel perfectly free in adopting this path, "baptizing" the method with the simple understanding that it is the indwelling Holy Spirit who is the agent of ongoing transformation and liberation.

The meditator starts out by following the inhalations and exhalations of one's breath. The teaching is that, at first, one silently counts the inhalations and exhalations, counting from one to ten, and then starting over again. This practice not only induces centering and inner calm, but also greatly helps prevent getting caught up in distractions or troublesome thoughts. When the meditator becomes aware that he or she is following a distraction, one simply continues counting, or starts over again at one. Eventually, after the practitioner has become comfortable and at ease with the Way of the Breath, the counting of the breath is abandoned. One simply follows the rhythm of the breath. There is a Buddhist teaching that one should become aware of the nostrils during the practice, the entrance and exit points of the breath. In time, the practice leads beyond awareness of the nostrils to an awareness of one's entire being—for the Christian, "resting in God," or simply "God."

If the Christian understands that the Hebrew word *ruah* means both "breath" and "spirit," our life force, then the intention of the meditator to be open to God's inward spirit and breath will maintain the Christian orientation of the practice. What opens out in time—like the leaves of the lotus flower—is an ever-deepening Christ-consciousness, of knowing God-in-Christ in the depths of one's being.

It is the heart that meditates, and love (will) is always at the core of any Christian meditation practice. If we live by the truth of our heart, and by love, "we shall grow in all ways into Christ" (Eph. 4:15).

Recommended to the reader are two books by Thich Naht Hanh: *Touching Peace: Practicing the Art of Mindful Living.* Berkeley, Calif.: Parallax Press, 1992.
Peace Is Every Step: The Path of Mindfulness in Everyday Life. Berkeley, Calif.: Parallax Press, 1993.

41   Lectio Divina

My words are Spirit and they are Life.
—John 6:63

Integral to the spiritual journey and fruitful meditation practice are the reading and absorption of scripture. The Buddhist must read the Sutras, the Hindu the Vedas and the Upanishads, the Muslim the Qur'an, and the Christian the Holy Bible. In Christianity, it is called *lectio divina.*

Lectio divina literally means "divine reading," as the reading of Holy Scripture was understood and practiced by the fourth–fifth-century Desert Fathers. For them, it also meant "divine listening," as they opened themselves in reflective silence to receive the illumination of the Holy Spirit as they searched the hidden or "mystical" (*mystikos* = hidden) meaning behind the written words. *Lectio divina* is understood as the prayerful, meditative, unhurried reading of scripture so that, by gift of grace, we experience the words of Christ: "My words are spirit and life" (John 6:63). It is the Holy Spirit who illumines us and reveals to us the deeper meanings and riches of scripture.

The Desert Fathers, as their chronicler John Cassian relates, understood that meditation on the scriptures is a "process which forms the soul . . . forming it after the likeness of God." Fruitful *lectio divina* calls for certain disciplines:

1. Before opening the Bible, we must ask God for the grace to reveal to us what we need to hear and understand in the depths of our hearts. A great teacher-saint of the early church wrote: "Do not approach the words of the mysteries contained in the Scriptures without prayer, asking for God's help. Consider prayer to be the key to understanding truth in Scripture" (St. Isaac the Syrian [seventh century]).

2. We should read short passages of scripture at one sitting, for each few sentences are rich in meaning and in grace. If we read

152

lengthy portions at one time, we will not fully grasp and assimilate everything we read. We may skirt the most important, grace-charged words that the Spirit wishes to communicate to us.

3. Scripture should be savored. This does not mean that we reflect on every sentence with equal note and reflectiveness, but that we take *none of the words of scripture for granted.* When certain passages deeply touch us, we should follow the lead of grace and "ponder these things in our heart" (Luke 2:52)—which usually means reflectively going back over the passage several times.

4. Biblical commentaries and exegesis are fine and helpful, but they are no substitute for the illuminating inspirations of the Holy Spirit. The Desert Fathers, most of whom were unlearned, understood that it is prayer that unlocks scripture. The mind does not penetrate these mysteries by learning or analysis, writes John Cassian, but is a gift–an illumination from on high. He says that our understanding of scripture will be proportionate to the purity of our hearts. As our spiritual life deepens, so does our understanding of the words of scripture. "Get to know the Scriptures by purity of heart, not by commentators," writes Cassian. The spiritual journey and *lectio divina* are intimately, inexorably bound together. *Indeed, there can be no spiritual journey without lectio divina.*

Origen, one of the earliest church fathers (185–252), was perhaps the greatest intellect of Christianity, including Aquinas and Augustine. Head of the famous school of Alexandria at the age of eighteen, he was the first great Christian interpreter of scripture. His teachings on the spiritual life shaped much of the early church, particularly monasticism and Eastern Orthodoxy. As Merton once remarked: "When you pronounce the name 'Origen', bow your head!"

Origen taught the importance of seeking the hidden (mystical) meaning behind the words of scripture, what the early Christians called "breaking open the word." He writes:

> The Scriptures were written by the Spirit of God, and have a meaning not only as is apparent at first sight, but also another which escapes notice of most. For these words which are written are the forms of certain mysteries, the image of divine things.[1]

While attending to the divine reading (*lectio divina*), seek with faith in God the hidden sense which is present in most passages of the divine scriptures. What is necessary for understanding divine things is prayer.[2]

How much *lectio divina* is called for? Many spiritual masters recommend that at least one hour a week be devoted to *lectio divina*—a half-hour at minimum.

Let us ask God to assist us through Jesus Christ by the Holy Spirit so that we may be able to unfold the mystical sense which is treasured up in the words before us.[3]

42   Invitation to the Dance

You and I are invited by the Mother to join the Evolutionary Dance, to glide *grace*-fully along the path that will lead us home to Eden. The dance is open to all who sincerely desire to participate and is closed to no one, only to those who have little faith, little love, little trust, and little courage. All we need do is learn the steps and become one with them and one with the Mother.

The steps are not complicated, but they do require practice and they call for a certain fortitude to keep us on the path, to keep us from falling off, for the path is high with many twists and turns. We must never look down or sneak a peek back, but always keep our eye on the horizon, beyond which is Eden, our home. Here the Divine Mother waits to embrace us, holding out her arms to enfold us.

What are the steps, you ask? If you have read this far, you already know what they are: The first step and the most important one—for it starts us on the path—is to meditate, to make meditation a daily task, our daily homage, if you will, to the Mother. How shall we find her unless we first find ourselves? How shall we recognize her until we have recognized ourselves, the person we truly are? The person we truly, deeply are is rooted in the Divine.

Step two is to learn to love unconditionally. This is the most difficult step of all, because it means cutting, sometimes ruthlessly, into the resilient fatty tissue of our egocentric selfish self. Remember the chapter about Peter, who could not love Jesus the way the Lord loved him? To be sure, each one of us is "Peter," and like Peter we need to be infused with Another's love if we are to love unconditionally, if we are to love the way Jesus loves us. There is no other way.

If we think we have our own little reservoir of love into which we can dip anytime the occasion demands, we will find our ladle quite muddy most times, not at all suitable for our neighbor. What neighbor is that, you ask? You know—the one with a personality that dri-

155

ves us up the wall, the one who is outwardly repugnant to our delicate sensitivities. You know—the one who is also *us!*

Step three is to become nonjudgmental, what Christ asked of us.
"Do not judge," he said. That's none of your business. Okay, so he
didn't add those specific words, but isn't that what he meant? Why
should we not judge? For one thing, we would be really judging ourselves, because our "shadow" projects our own hidden faults and fail-
ings on others, faults we refuse to recognize and accept as our own.
That "plank" we see in our neighbor's eye is *ours.* Unless, of course,
you believe that you are the one person on earth without a dark side,
without a shadow.

Step four is to practice mindfulness, to be present to the present,
to the now-moments of life. During those times when we are mindful,
we already are in the fourth dimension, the "eternal" now transcends
"clock time."

There are other steps to the dance we must learn, some of which
are obvious but easy to forget and overlook. The cosmic dance of evolution cannot be entered into unless we become forgiving people, for
mercy and forgiveness are prerequisites for being invited by the
Mother to her dance. She is continually forgiving us our countless,
often egregious trespasses. Why is it sometimes so difficult for us to
forgive others? We must try harder to forget about who is right and
who is wrong, work more at overlooking our little (and not so little)
hurt feelings. True love doesn't concern itself with such things. The
longer we insist on remaining babies, needing to be comforted and
suckled almost every moment, the more we risk getting pushed off
the dance floor.

We must also try to learn to be open to the whole world—open to
the truth of other spiritual paths and other wisdoms and other peoples. We must somehow learn to see "transparently"—to see into the
heart of things as they truly are, not one-dimensionally and opaquely
as if we were still third-dimensional people. Remember Jean Gebser's
words—we can no longer think and act as did our fathers and forefathers. The practice of meditation helps us to see deeply and not
superficially. Meditation opens our "inner eye" and allows us to see
the transparency and reality of things. To repeat: the universe and all
creation are open. Only *we* are closed.

There are other steps to master, but these will come naturally as we learn the main steps of the dance. Oh, yes—the dance often includes one step forward and two steps back! That's okay, nothing to be concerned about. Life is an ebb and flow, a tide that comes in and recedes. If we think for a moment that all our steps are going to be faultless, carrying us unhesitatingly always forward, then we haven't learned even the fundamental steps of the dance.

We do not have much time to join the evolutionary dance; this dance that moves to the music of the spheres, that will go on with or without us. This is a dance that can end rather abruptly if enough of us do not join in and participate. Mother Earth is writhing and dying before our eyes. She is approaching her death throes. Who would ever watched their mother die and not do something to save her if they could?

Let us join the great evolutionary dance, for join we must. It is the last dance on the card. It is the Mother's dance, and she is saving it for us. After the last dance is over and we head for the doors, will we walk into hell or into a new world? Will we have to start all over again and dig our way out of the charred rubble and burning debris of a world we ourselves destroyed? Or shall we have taken the Mother's outstretched hand and, with unbounded trust, allow her to lead us into our destiny—our return to Eden.

> Lord let your thunder strike
> into the prison of false religion,
> And bring to this unhappy land
> the light of Knowledge.
>
> —Tagore

 *Epilogue*

Evolution presses on toward the increasing perfection of man, which should be understood in an anthropological and not in a moral sense. This process never reverses itself, and we are not even asked if we want what is coming. It just happens, and religions, too, must honor this. They must join with it and reorient themselves toward it. When a religion fails to allow this, it will not survive, even though it may vegetate for a while longer with a few adherents. With the new consciousness, man will become a mystic. The new man will stand on a higher step than man of the mental structure. This step will have a significance in human development second only to the evolution from animal to man.

—Enomiya-Lassalle[1]

 **Notes**

PART I: THE DAWN OF THE MYSTICAL AGE

1. Jean Gebser, *The Ever-Present Origen* (Athens, Oh.: Ohio University Press, 1984), 300.

1. Home, Home to Eden

1. Rabindranath Tagore (1861–1941) is the greatest of India's Bengali poets; also an educator and social reformer. All cited excerpts of the poems of Tagore are from *The Later Poems of Tagore*, trans. Aurobindo Bose (New York: Funk & Wagnalls, 1976).
2. Tibetan Master Sogyal Rinpoche as cited in *Dialogues with a Modern Mystic: An Interview with Andrew Harvey* (Wheaton, Ill.: Quest Books, 1994), 33.
3. Ken Wilber, *Sex, Ecology, Spirituality* (Boston, Mass.: Shambhala Press, 1995),1:258.
4. Sri Aurobindo, *The Human Cycle, The Essential Aurobindo*, ed. Robert E. McDermott (Hudson, N.Y.: Landisfarne Press, 1987), iii. *Biographical note:* Sri Aurobindo (1872–1950) stands as the single most accomplished yogi of modern India, exemplifying an ideal blend of spiritual attainment and socio-political activism. He was highly critical of the Buddhist view of the denial of a permanent self.

2. Humanity on the Precipice

1. Karl Jaspers, *The Future of Mankind* (Chicago, Ill.: University of Chicago Press, 1961), 8.
2. Gebser, *The Ever-Present*, 298.
3. Jaspers, *The Future*, viii.
4. Sri Aurobindo, *The Essential*, 192.
5. Ibid., 193.
6. Ibid., 191.
7. Jaspers, *The Future*, 342.

3. Out of the Darkness

1. Hugo Enomiya-Lassalle, S.J., *Living in the New Consciousness* (Boston, Mass.: Shambhala Press, 1986), 29.

2. Gebser, *The Ever-Present,* 294.
3. Enomiya-Lassalle, *Living,* 61.
4. Ibid., 61.
5. Gebser, *The Ever-Present,* 283.
6. Wilber, *Sex, Ecology,* 1:ix.

4. Image and Likeness

1. Enomiya-Lassalle, *Living,* 4.
2. Gebser, *The Ever-Present,* 2.
3. George A. Maloney, S.J., introduction to my book *Why Not Be a Mystic?* (New York: Crossroad, 1995), 13.
4. Enomiya-Lassalle, *Living,* 29.
5. Ibid., 35.
6. Sri Aurobindo, *Savitri: A Legend and a Symbol, The Essential Aurobindo,* 219.

5. A New River

1. Enomiya-Lassalle, *Living,* 11.
2. Fahkruddin 'Iraqi, *Divine Flashes.* All cited excerpts from the poetry of Fahkruddin 'Iraqi are from The Classics of Western Spirituality series (Mahwah, N.J.: Paulist Press, 1985). *Biographical note:* 'Iraqi was a Persian writer and poet of the thirteenth-century, living at the peak of the revival of Islamic spirituality.
3. Enomiya-Lassalle, *Living,* 140.
4. Ibid., 141.
5. Karl Rahner, *The Shape of the Church to Come* (New York: Seabury Press, 1971), 57.
6. Ibid., 24.
7. Origen (185–252?), *Letter to Gregory, Bishop of Caesarea,* The Ante-Nicene Fathers (Peabody, Mass.: Hendrickson Publishers, 1995), 9:296. *Biographical note:* Origen is one of the greatest of the Church Fathers and considered by many the greatest intellect of Christianity, including Augustine and Aquinas. He was the first great Christian interpreter and textual exegete of Scripture. Appointed head of the famous Catechetical School of Alexandria at the age of eighteen, Origen profoundly influenced the early Eastern Church, particularly later monasticism. Merton once remarked: "When you pronounce the name 'Origen,' bow your head!"
8. Enomiya-Lassalle, *Living,* 142.
9. Gebser, *The Ever-Present,* 11.

6. Signs of the Now-Present Future

1. Harvey, *Dialogues,* 59.
2. Sri Aurobindo, *The Essential,* 215.

7. The Present Great Planet Earth

1. Jaspers, *The Future*, 2.
2. Rachel Carson, *Silent Spring* (New York: Houghton, Mifflin & Co., 1958), 63.
3. Chief Seattle's speech when he was asked to sell tribal lands to the U.S. government. *Power to the People: Active Non-Violence in the U.S.* (Culver City, Calif.: Peace Press, 1977), 9.
4. Gebser, *The Ever-Present,* 311.
5. Maloney, *Mysticism and the New Age* (New York: Alba House, 1991), 39.
6. Harvey, *Dialogues,* 57.

8. A Divided Consciousness

1. Bede Griffiths, OSB, *The Marriage of East and West* (Springfield, Ill.: Templegate Publishers, 1982), 113.
2. Thomas Merton, *New Seeds of Contemplation* (New York: New Directions, 1961), 35.
3. Ibid., *The Inner Experience* (Spencer, Mass.: Cistercian Publications, 1983–84). Offset of an unpublished manuscript which Merton worked on during the last six years of his life. A codicil in Merton's will prevents it from being published as a book. The Merton Legacy Trust gave permission to Cistercian Publications to serialize an edited version of the manuscript over eight quarterly issues, 1983–84.
4. Sri Ramakrishna, *The Gospel of Ramakrishna,* trans. Swami Nikhilananda (New York: Ramakrishna-Vivekananda Center Publishing, 1984), 177. *Biographical note:* Sri Ramakrishna is an acknowledged great saint and sage of nineteenth-century India (1836–1886). He was a priest of the Dakshineswar Temple on the sacred Ganges River where God is worshiped as the Mother of the Universe.

9. The Concentration Camp of Reason

1. Harvey, *Dialogues,* 32.
2. Ibid., 51.
3. Novalis was the pseudonym of the late-eighteenth-century German poet Friedrich von Hardenberg (1772–1801), who died at the age of 29.

10. Owning Our Shadow

1. Robert A. Johnson, *Owning Your Own Shadow* (San Francisco: Harper Collins, 1991), 21.
2. Ibid., 7, 42.
3. Carl Jung, *Collected Works* (Princeton, N.J.: Princeton University Press, 1957–72), 8:9. Jung understood the shadow as "personifying everything that the subject refuses to acknowledge about himself or herself, and yet is always thrusting itself upon others, directly or indirectly—for instance, inferior traits of character."
4. Johnson, *Owning,* 17.

PART 2: THE SACRED FEMININE

11. Hagia Sophia

1. Thomas Merton, *Hagia Sophia,* The Collected Poems of Thomas Merton (New York: New Directions, 1977), 363.
2. Ibid., 369.
3. Harvey, *Dialogues,* 3.
4. Merton, *Hagia,* 65.

12. Death of a Mystic

1. Bede Griffiths, *Discovering the Feminine* (Sidney, Australia: More Than Illusion Films video tape, 1993). *Biographical note:* At the age of 56, Bede Griffiths left his Benedictine Abbey of Farnborough, England, where he had been Prior, and went to India where he assisted in the foundation of Kurisumala Ashram, a monastery of the Syrian Rite, in Kerala, India. Thirteen years later he came with two monks to Saccidananda Ashram in Tamil Nadu, southern India, where he would spend the rest of his life, except for travels around the world. His life was a life of prayer, asceticism, simplicity, writing and teaching. He lived as a Hindu, absorbing its culture and its scriptures, in which he found great treasures which threw light on his own Christian scriptures and journey. He died May 13,1993. From the surrounding villages, some far away, Christians, Hindus, Muslims, and Buddhists came to offer their final respects to this saintly seeker of God.
2. Eyewitness account by Andrew Harvey, cited in *Dialogues,* 28.
3. Griffiths, *River of Compassion* (Warwick, N.Y.: Amity House, 1987), 175.

13. The Mother

1. Julian of Norwich, as cited by Andrew Harvey, *Dialogues,* 57.
2. Harvey, *Dialogues,* 70.
3. Ibid., 70.
4. Ibid., 75.
5. Ibid., 77.
6. Ibid., 78.

14. Womb of Our Rebirth

1. Martin Buber, *The Way of the Jewish Mystics,* ed. Perle Besserman (Boston, Mass.: Shambhala Press, 1994), 66.
2. Yves Raguin, S.J., *Paths to Contemplation* (Wheatherstead, England: Anthony Clarke Press, 1987), 27.
3. John A. Sanford, *Mystical Christianity* (New York: Crossroad, 1994), 334.

4. Thomas Merton, *Zen and the Birds of Appetite* (New York: New Directions, 1968), 76.

15. The Mystic and the Sacred Feminine

1. Harvey, *Dialogues*, 38.
2. Jung, *Answer to Job*, Collected Works, 2:377.
3. Thomas Merton, *The Inner Experience* (Spencer, Mass., Cistercian Studies, 1983), 19:273.
4. Meister Eckhart, as cited by George A. Maloney, *Mary The Womb of God* (Denville, N.J.: Dimension Books, 1976), 23.

16. The Souls of Our Children

1. Enomiya-Lassalle, *Living*, 35.

17. Experiment in the Ever-Present Future

1. Sri Aurobindo, *The Essential*, 225–26.
2. Ibid., 238.
3. Tagore, *The Later Poems.*
4. Sri Aurobindo, *The Essential*, 244.
5. Ibid., 240. "The Mother" (formerly Mira Richard, a French-Algerian citizen) was Sri Aurobindo's closest disciple. He once said of her: "The Mother's consciousness and mine are the same."

PART 3: CHARACTERISTICS OF THE NEW CONSCIOUSNESS

18. Recovery of the Sacred

1. Merton, *The Inner*, 18:214–15.

19. Living Time-Free

1. Enomiya-Lassalle, *Living*, 32.
2. Ibid., 12.
3. Ibid., 32.
4. While the "Big Bang Theory" remains a theory, it has gained much credibility in the scientific world since it was first proposed. Radio telescopes have recorded the "hiss" of the "big bang" event, while the Hubble telescope has peered more than ten billion years into space. Astronomers believe the telescope will one day record the "big bang" of some fifteen billion years ago.
5. Enomiya-Lassalle, *Living*, 9.

20. The New Thinking

1. Enomiya-Lassalle, *Living*, 18.
2. Jaspers, *The Future*, 217.
3. Ibid., 204.

21. A New Church

1. Harvey, *Dialogues*, 37.
2. Sanford, *Mystical*, 152.
3. Maloney, *Inscape*, privately distributed teachings on prayer.
4. Enomiya-Lassalle, *Living*, 13.
5. Ibid., 141.
6. Jung, *Collected Works*, 10:495.
7. Idem, *The Undiscovered Self,* Collected Works, 10:493.
8. Rahner, *The Shape*, 85.
9. Enomiya-Lassalle, *Living*, 133.
10. Rahner, *The Shape*, 45.

22. The Fall of Fundamentalism

1. Flo Conway, *Holy Terror: The Fundamentalist War on America's Freedoms* (New York: Doubleday, 1982), 199.
2. *National Catholic Reporter,* August 9, 1996, 13.
3. Origin, *De Principiis,* Ante-Nicene Fathers, 4:241.
4. Thomas Merton, *Bread in the Wilderness* (New York: New Directions, 1953), 28, 37.
5. Raymond E. Brown, *The Community of the Beloved Disciple* (New York: Paulist Press, 1985), 15.
6. Ibid., 20.
7. D. Bruce Lockerbie, *Billy Sunday* (Waco, Tex.: Word Books, 1965), 63.

23. All Things Inter-Are

1. Angelus Silesius, *Western Classics of Spirituality* (Mahwah, N.J.: Paulist Press, 1986), 97.
2. "Myth" is to be understood not in the sense of fairytale or fabrication, but in the classic sense such as used by mythologist Joseph Campbell, i.e., a story that veils a truth.
3. Leo D. Lefebure, *The Buddha and the Christ* (Maryknoll, N.Y.: Orbis Books, 1993), 158–59.
4. Nehunia Ben Hakanah, *The Way of the Jewish Mystics,* 57.
5. Sri Ramakrishna, *The Gospel of Ramakrishna,* 177.

24. Wedding Bells

1. *The Gospel of Thomas,* The Nag Hammadi Library, ed. James M. Robinson (Englewood Cliffs, N.J.: Prentice Hall, 1990), no. 22. The *Gospel of Thomas* is considered authentic by several highly respected biblical scholars. It is a col-

lection of 114 sayings, proverbs, prophecies, and parables of Jesus, translated from the Greek about 200 C.E. The original Greek, and perhaps the original Aramaic or Syriac manuscripts, may have been composed as early as the second half of the first century. Its authorship is ascribed to Didymos Judas Thomas (Judas the Twin), an apostle closely identified with the early Syriac Church.
2. Harvey, *Dialogues*, 58.
3. Maloney, *Mysticism*, 127.
4. Ibid., 128.
5. Jung, *Man and His Symbols* (New York: Dell Publishing, 1964), 4.

26. Radical Detachment

I. Cf. my book *Why Not Be a Mystic?* 92–114.
2. Angelus Silesius, *Western Classics*, 76.

27. The Forgotten Virtue

1. Western Christianity has devised three general classifications of the virtues: theological, cardinal, and moral. Each category is subdivided into lesser, but nonetheless important, virtues. The moral virtues are further nuanced by dividing them into acquired and infused. With a ruler and a pen, one can even make an neat chart of it all to graphically demonstrate what has been called "the spiritual organism," which, following St. Thomas, goes on to define the corresponding seven gifts of the Holy Spirit. Such a delineation is a prime example of neo-scholastic left-brain thinking, a construct based on Aristotelian thought processes. It should be noted that the Eastern Church, ever wary of defining things too meticulously, has no such comparable neat edifice of the virtues.
2. Thich Naht Hanh, *Living Buddha, Living Christ* (New York: Riverhead Books, 1995), 16.
3. Ibid., 16.

28. The Emergence of Women

1. Wilber, *Sex, Ecology*, 162.
2. Ibid., 157.
3. Ibid., 159.
4. Ibid., 158.
5. Thomas Merton, *Springs of Contemplation* (New York: Farrar, Strauss, 1992), 161–62.
6. Wilber, *Sex, Ecology*, 162.

29. Swords Into Plowshares

1. Jaspers, *The Future*, 80.
2. Ibid., 232.
3. Ibid.

PART 4: MEDITATION: DOOR TO THE NEW CONSCIOUSNESS

30. The Challenge of Everyday Life

1. Raguin, *Paths,* 25.
2. Ibid., 21.

31. Search for the True Self

1. Merton, *The Inner,* 1:5.
2. Ibid., *New Seeds,* 51.
3. Ibid., *The Inner,* 1:5.
4. Ibid., *New Seeds,* 25.
5. Ibid., *The Inner,* 1:5-6.
6. Abraham Maslow, "From the Peak to the Plateau Experience," *Journal of Transpersonal Psychology* 27 (1995): 1.

32. Death Is Transfiguration

1. Rumi (d. 1273) is the greatest of the Persian Sufi poets. He is regarded by all the great spiritual traditions as a great saint and sage. His poetry ranks among the world's most sublime expressions of unitive love with the Divine.
2. Origen, *Commentary on the Gospel of John,* Ante-Nicene Fathers Series, 9:303.
3. Sogyal Rinpoche (d. 1987), *The Tibetan Book of Living and Dying* (San Francisco: HarperCollins, 1992), 151. *Biographical note:* Great Tibetan meditation master and teacher of Dzogchen (pronounced Zug-Chen) which is considered the highest teaching of the Buddha. (In the Kagnu lineage it is known as Mahamudra.) Dzogchen is considered the greatest vehicle of self-liberation, often referred to as "insight meditation," because this discipline penetrates all veils and illusions and goes to "pure reality," or "naked awareness." It is called "Atiyoga," known as The Great Perfection.
4. Merton, *The Asian Journal of Thomas Merton* (New York: New Directions, 1973), 343. Conclusion of his opening address to the First Asian Congress of Religious in Bangkok, Thailand, December 10, 1968. Returning to his room at the Red Cross complex, he took a shower, stepped from the shower and attempted to turn off an electric stand fan. He touched exposed wiring and was electrocuted, causing a massive heart attack.

33. Right Meditation

1. Anonymous, *The Cloud of Unknowing,* The Classics of Western Spirituality (Mahwah, N.J.: Paulist Press, 1981),130.
2. Rahner, *On Prayer* (Paramus, N.J.: Paulist Press, 1958), 52.

34. Right Understanding

1. Ken Wilber, *Up From Eden* (Garden City, N.Y.: Anchor Press, 1981), 321.

2. Merton, *The Inner*, 1:9.
3. Ibid., 5:76.
4. William Johnston, S.J., *Being in Love* (London: Fount Paperbacks, 1988), 47.
5. Pseudo-Dionysius, *The Mystical Theology*, The Classics of Western Spirituality (Mahwah, N.J.: Paulist Press, 1987), 135.

35. Right Attitude

1. John Cassian, *Tenth Conference*, The Classics of Western Spirituality (Mahwah, N.J.: Paulist Press, 1985), 128–29.
2. Ibid., 102.
3. Ibid., 103.
4. John Ruysbroeck, *The Spiritual Espousals*, The Classics of Western Spirituality (Mahwah, N.J.: Paulist Press, 1985), 151.

PART V: WAYS OF CHRISTIAN CONTEMPLATIVE MEDITATION

1. Vladimir Lossky, *The Mystical Theology of the Orthodox Church* (Crestwood, N.Y.: St. Vladimir Press, 1976), 208.
2. Thomas Keating, OCSO, letter to me, July 11, 1996.
3. Teresa of Avila, *The Way of Perfection* (Washington, D.C.: ICS Publications, 1980), 142.

36. The Way of the Mantra

1. John Cassian, *Tenth Conference*, 136.
2. Ibid., 131.
3. Swami Muktananda was head of the Hindu Siddha lineage until he died in 1981. The Siddha mantra—Om Namah Shivaya (I honor the Divine within)—is considered, as are all sacred mantras, as *chaitanya*, or alive, with the power to awaken the inner meditative energy called *kundalini*. It is taught that once this potential is awakened, silent meditation occurs spontaneously and spiritual evolution accelerates naturally.
4. John Main, *Word Into Silence* (Ramsey, N.J.: Paulist Press, 1980), 15.
5. Ibid., 14.

37. The Way of The Jesus Prayer

1. Theophane the Recluse, as cited in *The Art of Prayer*, trans. E. Kadloubovsky and G. E. H. Palmer (London: Faber & Faber, 1966), 190–91. *Biographical note:* Theophane (1815–1894) was a Russian bishop who later became a hermit. He is one of the greatest teachers of The Jesus Prayer and is a saint of the Russian Orthodox Church.
2. Merton, *New Seeds*, 37.
3. Pseudo-Macarius, *The Fifty Spiritual Homilies*, trans. George A. Maloney, The Classics of Western Spirituality (Mahwah, N.J.: Paulist Press, 1992), 116. *Biographical note:* Macarius was a fourth-century Syrian monk, one of several

well-known personages with the name "Macarius." His precise identity is not possible; therefore, he is referred to as Pseudo-Macarius.

4. *The Philokalia* (love of the beautiful), trans. E. Kadloubovsky and G. E. H. Palmer (London: Faber & Faber, 1973), is a most revered work of Eastern Orthodoxy, a collection of the writings of the Fathers of Hesychast spirituality and the theology and practice of The Jesus Prayer, or "prayer of the heart."
5. Theophane, *The Art,* 198.
6. Thomas Merton, Letter to Fr. Fidelis, OCSO, The School of Charity Letters (New York: Farrar, Straus & Giroux, 1990), 176–77.
7. Kallistos Ware, *The Art,* 28.
8. Bishop Ignatius Brianchaninov, *On the Prayer of Jesus* (London: John M. Watkins Publishing, 1965), 8.

38. The Way of Centering Prayer

1. Anonymous, *The Cloud,* 120.
2. Ibid., 124.
3. Thomas Keating, *Open Mind, Open Heart* (New York: Continuum, 1995), 3–4.

39. The Way of Zen

1. Thomas Merton, *Zen and the Birds of Appetite* (New York: New Directions, 1968), 3.
2. Ibid., 3.
3. Ibid., 38.
4. Enomiya-Lassalle, *The Practice of Zen Meditation* (San Francisco: Aquarian Press, 1990), 72.

40. The Way of the Breath

1. Thich Naht Hanh, *Touching Peace: Practicing the Art of Mindful Living* (Berkeley, Calif.: Parallax Press, 1992), 1.

41. Lectio Divina

1. Origen, *De Principiis,* Ante-Nicene Fathers, 4:241.
2. Ibid., *Letter to Gregory,* Ante-Nicene Fathers, 9:296.
3. Ibid., *Commentary on the Gospel of John,* Ante-Nicene Fathers, 9:305.

Epilogue

1. Enomiya-Lassalle, *Living,* 133.